EF 173355
£15.00

Punishment and the Punished

Punishment
and
the Punished

Lord Longford

CHAPMANS
1991

Chapmans Publishers Ltd
141–143 Drury Lane
London WC2B 5TB

BRITISH LIBRARY CATALOGUING IN PUBLICATION DATA
Longford, Frank Pakenham, Earl of, *1905–*
Punishment and the punished.
1. Great Britain. Criminal law. Justice. Administration
I. Title
364.941

ISBN 1–85592–527–3

First published by Chapmans 1991
Reprinted 1991

Photoset in Linotron Baskerville by Rowland Phototypesetting Ltd
Bury St Edmunds, Suffolk

Printed and bound in Great Britain by
Butler & Tanner Ltd, Frome and London

To Elizabeth

Acknowledgements

In writing this book and in the work that has led up to it over so many years, I have received a vast amount of help from men and women whom I can only thank in a collective sense. Naturally I am especially grateful to all those who allowed me to interview them and who contributed so much to any value the book possesses.

Gwen Keeble, as so often, has been my closest ally. I am also very grateful to Barbara Winch, Kitty Chapman, Jenny Mackilligin, Jane Davies, the very efficient staff of the St Stephen's Secretariat, and to Matthew Oliver.

Contents

INTRODUCTION   **The Penal Crisis** 1

My Penal Experience 8

PART I   **Administrators of Justice**

Lord Windlesham 19
*Former Minister of State at the Home Office
and Former Chairman of the Parole Board*

Lord Hunt of Llanfair Waterdine .. 22
Former Chairman of the Parole Board

Judge Stephen Tumim 26
Her Majesty's Chief Inspector of Prisons

Lord Allen of Abbeydale 30
*Former Permanent Under-Secretary of State at
the Home Office*

Mary Tuck 39
*Former Head of the Home Office Research and
Planning Unit*

The Revd Peter Timms 49
Former Governor of Maidstone Prison

David Evans 57
*General Secretary of the Prison Officers'
Association*

Alan Eastwood 61
Chairman of the Police Federation

PART II   **Penal Reformers**

Peter Thompson 67
*Founder and Director of the Matthew Trust
for Mental Patients and Victims of Crime*

Professor Terence Morris 73
*Professor of Social Institutions at the
University of London*

Paul Cavadino 79
*National Association for the Care and
Resettlement of Offenders*

Stephen Shaw 85
Director of the Prison Reform Trust

Harry Fletcher 89
*Assistant General Secretary of the National
Association of Probation Officers*

Eric McGraw 93
Director of the New Bridge for Ex-Prisoners

Edward Fitzgerald 96
Barrister at Law

Christopher Holtom 103
*Vice-President of the National Association of
Victim Support Schemes*

A Joint Manifesto for Penal Reform   113

PART III   **The Punished**

**The Guildford Four and the
Maguire Family Group** 117

Chris Tchaikovsky 122
Founder and Director of Women in Prison

Michael Bettsworth 129
*Former Headmaster Convicted of Sexual
Offences*

Rosie Johnston 132
Served a Prison Sentence for Drugs Offences

Kim Wan 142
Former Cat Burglar and Inmate of Dartmoor

John Masterson 145
*Former Violent Offender and Inmate of the
Wakefield Control Unit*

PART IV   **Punishment and the Punished**

I   Provisional Reflections 155
II   Sentencing 157
III   Five Crucial Issues 163
IV   The Idea of Punishment 180
V   Retribution 185
VI   Punishment and Christian
      Theology 189
VII Conclusions 194

Select Bibliography 198

Index 201

Introduction: The Penal Crisis

The riots at Strangeways prison in April 1990 were nearly at an
end when I paid a flying visit. Six prisoners were still on the roof.
The *Sun* newspaper had printed a cartoon of these prisoners
watching a decrepit old man as he made his way towards the wall
of the prison. 'It's worse than the SAS,' said one of them. 'They've
arranged a visit from Lord Longford.' As I was escorted round the
prison, slates began descending from above. 'They know you've
arrived,' said the Assistant Governor to me sardonically.

But the riot was no joking matter. Two men, one a prison
officer, one a prisoner, had died. A number of prisoners had been
brutally assaulted by other prisoners. The Governor, a devout
Christian held in the highest esteem throughout the prison
service, referred to 'an explosion of evil'. With particular support
from the prison chaplains, he had been introducing improvements recently. A representative of the prison officers described
the behaviour of some of the prisoners as that of animals.

Another angle was provided for me by a former Strangeways
prisoner. What follows was written before the outbreak:

> The atmosphere in Strangeways is always very tense, and any
> of a variety of events could trigger off violent outbursts. It is
> extremely dehumanizing to live in such conditions, with little
> idea of the outside world. Lack of diversion means that prison-
> ers are constantly thinking about their crimes, their resent-
> ment, their conditions and their future.
>
> When locked up for long periods with other inmates,
> criminal notes are compared and relationships inevitably
> formed. These may be of hatred further fuelling tension, or of
> camaraderie, in which case plans are made for future 'jobs',
> revenge attacks and so on.

Clifford Longley of *The Times* was equally severe on Strangeways in an article published on 9 June 1990, under the heading 'Hotbeds of Hatred':

The ritual stripping of personal clothing, possessions and title conveys a powerful psychological message of worthlessness. Even the notorious practice of slopping out underlines the denial of dignity, and hence powerlessness, of the prisoner. The message the prisoner was once intended to draw from his treatment was that he is nothing, because God is all. The message he now derives from it is that he is nothing, and that is all. It is a message of hopelessness.

When it was built in the nineteenth century, Strangeways prison was intended for 970 prisoners. Living standards generally have improved out of all recognition since then. A much smaller number of prisoners might have seemed appropriate. In fact, there were 1600 at the time of the riots. I have often been asked whether I foresaw any such thing happening. Not on that scale perhaps, but I had long felt that some explosion was inevitable. The riots at Strangeways were, of course, copied in other prisons.

To explain is not to excuse. Nothing can excuse the horrifying violence displayed. But that does not prevent us as a community from accepting our responsibility for the conditions that led up to it. I refer below (page 57) to the grim statement of a crisis made in evidence to me *before* the riots by the General Secretary of the Prison Officers' Association. I refer also to the deterioration in prison conditions over the last thirty-five years mentioned by a former prison governor, the Reverend Peter Timms, and a leading criminologist, Professor Terence Morris. Some of us have for so long been crying wolf that our warnings were liable to be discounted. But now (pun permitted) a Lord Justice Woolf has been urgently called upon by the government not only to investigate the Strangeways riots but also to examine the whole penal situation. It would be difficult to deny today the existence of a prison crisis.

In an article in the *Guardian* of 27 April 1990, Roy King, Professor of Social Theory and Institutions at the University of

Wales, Bangor, described the findings of research conducted by himself and his colleague, Dr Kathy McDermott. Among the aspects of life at Strangeways, he referred to the lamentable shortage of work:

Even on the most optimistic interpretation of the figures, the improvements in hours which prisoners spent at work, for example, brought Strangeways up to 70 per cent of what Winchester prison achieved in 1972 – regarded at the time as unacceptably low.

More generally, Professor King reported: 'Our research demonstrated a massive deterioration in prison regime in all types of prisons for adult males during the past twenty years. . . . What the Home Office must face is that potentially every prison is vulnerable.'

Dr Robert Runcie, until recently Archbishop of Canterbury, in a notable pamphlet (April 1990) laid emphasis on the 1988 report of the Chief Inspector of Prisons, a document which I found very depressing. He saw signs of recent improvement, as did the Reverend Peter Timms (see page 52). But both were equally severe in their overall criticism of the present situation. One of the key passages in Dr Runcie's pamphlet should be quoted in full:

Humanity is difficult to achieve in overcrowded cells, where many are confined for most of their working hours, where the routines are numbing and repetitive for prisoner and prison officer alike, where the indignity and squalor of slopping out are likely to remain until at least the end of the century, where visiting hours for loved ones are still severely restricted in many cases. In such conditions it is difficult to hold on to humanity, let alone extend it.

The Archbishop refers with sorrow to 'the current rejection of the rehabilitative ideal'.

Baroness Blackstone, Master of Birkbeck College and Chairman of a crucial Labour Party Policy Committee, has written a scathing attack on the British prison system as it is today, with which I agree in essence. Her booklet, *Prisons and Penal Reform* (1990), starts in arresting style:

> Britain's prisons are institutions of which we should be ashamed. They are absurdly expensive, yet scandalously inhumane. For the most part they are in old or decrepit buildings, but even where the buildings are new, they are badly designed. They absorb large amounts of manpower, yet typically lock inmates in their cells for many hours a day. They are overcrowded and unhygienic. They enforce idleness and encourage helplessness. They certainly punish; they hardly reform.

Lady Blackstone naturally refers to well-known facts often mentioned in these pages:

> The number of people we incarcerate in these dreadful institutions has grown year by year. We now have a considerably higher proportion of our population in prison than all our European neighbours, exceeding not just Scandinavia, France, Belgium, Holland and Germany, but even Spain, Portugal, Greece and Turkey. Our detention rate is proportionately well over twice as high as that of some other countries in Europe.

Lady Blackstone is as aware as anyone of the remorseless increase in crime. When I first visited prisoners just before the war, there were 10,000 people in prison. Since then the figure has touched 50,000. By and large the increase in crime has been responsible, and with it has come an increase in public distaste for prisoners (see the table opposite). It should be noted that the government admitted quite recently that the higher proportion of the population in prison in Britain cannot be attributed to higher rates of crime than in Europe.

This is not the place to describe in detail either Lady Blackstone's analysis or her remedies. But again and again she returns to sentencing issues:

> Sentencing policy is the key to reducing the numbers in prison.

Imprisonment in Western Europe

Country	Prison population on 1.9.1988	Number of prisoners per 100,000 population
United Kingdom	55,457	97.4
Turkey	51,810	95.6
Luxembourg	322	86.5
West Germany	52,076	84.9
Portugal	8,181	83.0
France	46,423	81.1
Austria	5,862	77.0
Spain	29,344	75.8
Switzerland	4,679	73.1
Finland	3,598	73.0
Denmark	3,469	68.0
Malta	221	67.0
Belgium	6,450	65.4
Italy	34,675	60.4
Sweden	4,716	56.0
Ireland	1,953	55.0
Norway	2,041	48.4
Greece	4,288	44.0
Holland	5,827	40.0
Cyprus	219	39.3
Iceland	89	35.6

The figure for the United Kingdom does not include 1511 prisoners, mostly unsentenced, who were held in police custody on that date.

Figures for the individual countries within the United Kingdom:

England and Wales	48,595	96.7
Scotland	5,076	99.3
Northern Ireland	1,786	114.2

Source: Statistics compiled by the Council of Europe, as on 1 September 1988.

It is also the key to improving prison conditions. Conditions deteriorate dramatically with overcrowding. Disgraceful local prisons like Reading cannot be closed while so many offenders are being given custodial sentences. However, other steps can be taken to mitigate some of the worst aspects of life in prison.

She elaborates some of these effectively. Except in regard to young adults and juveniles, she considers that the courts possess far too much discretion over sentencing which, sadly, they have misused. The great failure of the government has been to refrain from imposing statutory restrictions upon this discretion.

Since Lady Blackstone's booklet was published, there has been a fail in the aggregate prison population after a long period of steady increase. Between November 1988 and November 1989, there was a reduction in the number of prisoners held in penal establishments from 49,340 to 48,154. But the fall was entirely due to the decline in the number of sentenced young offenders and remand prisoners. The number of sentenced adults increased slightly, and it seems to be assumed that it will go on increasing. A Home Office projection of the prison population published *after* the issue of the government White Paper *Crime, Justice and Protecting the Public* in February 1990 pointed to an increase of 12,000 to 61,200 by 1997–8 (see page 162 below). The figures were later revised downwards to an increase of 7500 by 1998.

The overcrowding is rightly picked upon as the most obvious feature of the present deplorable situation. In February 1990 10,556 prisoners were doubled up in cells designed for one, while 3333 were sharing three to a cell. Leeds prison was 95 per cent overcrowded, Bedford 88 per cent overcrowded, Birmingham 75 per cent, Leicester 72 per cent, Strangeways (on 31 March 1990) 65 per cent. Overall, we are told, the system was only 5.3 per cent overcrowded, but that is a small consolation to the staff and prisoners in such prisons as those mentioned.

This is not a book against punishment or even against prisons, although I am profoundly convinced that we make use of both of them much too often and much too harshly. A good many years ago, Mr Gilbert Hare, then a distinguished Governor of Strangeways, gave a talk which began in this way:

> Yes, I am the governor of a prison. In your eyes there is no doubt that nothing can be said for prisons. You may prefer capital punishment, mutilation, transportation, public humiliation in the stocks or a good flogging. All of these recipes have been used in the past without obvious success. If you don't want any of them, you may find yourself falling back on prison as the

least evil way, indeed a necessary way, of coping with those who commit crime.

Since that time, there has been a large (though not large enough) use of alternatives to prison. Governor Hare might not give precisely the same talk today, but the problem he placed before us then remains with us.

This book finally goes to press on 14 December 1990. It seems likely that before it can be published the Woolf Report will have been handed to the government. It is possible that the publication of that Report will precede the publication of this book. Certainly, we already have a new Prime Minister and Cabinet.

I shall be much surprised if the Woolf Report does not contain radical proposals for improving our prison system. This seems to be all the more likely because I gather that Judge Stephen Tumim, Her Majesty's Chief Inspector of Prisons, will be joint author. He has already produced a series of scathing reports on the state of our prisons, including an indictment of the conditions in Leeds prison which led to a number of suicides. His general report on suicide in prison, just published, is damning.

The most important event since the bulk of this book was completed has been the publication of the government's Criminal Justice Bill, a major event by any reckoning. NACRO (National Association for the Care and Resettlement of Offenders) have already circulated their own assessment of a Bill 'containing some valuable reforms but marred by a few objectionable measures'. There is only space here for me to offer strong support to four of NACRO's criticisms: 1) The power given to courts to give violent or sexual offenders sentences longer than the offence deserves if the court considers this 'necessary to protect the public from serious harm from the offender'; 2) The suggestion of private management of remand centres; 3) The failure to establish a Sentencing Council; and 4) The failure to introduce the code of standards for prisons.

So much is background. Before we reach conclusions, let us hear from a number of those who, for one reason or another, are worth listening to about punishments and prisons. But first, a summarized account of my own penal experience.

My Penal Experience

When I am asked how I first came to take an interest in prisoners, now half a century ago, I give a rather vague answer. In 1936 I became a member of the Labour Party and a City Councillor in Oxford, having served some years previously in the Conservative Party Research Department. I was obsessed with a desire to help those in greatest need and, in order to help them, to understand them. It was an easy step, physically and psychologically, to call at Oxford prison on the way from Christ Church, where I was a tutor, to the station.

The war suspended my prison visiting. I renewed it in 1945, but was soon transported to a minor role in the government. When that government came to an end in 1951, I looked for a solid piece of social investigation. I was privileged to obtain an invitation from the Nuffield Foundation to conduct a two-year inquiry into the *Causes of Crime*, published as a book in 1958.

In the course of that inquiry, I visited fifteen prisons, six Borstals, three Remand Homes and two Approved Schools. I met countless prisoners and then or later came to know a number of them well. When I pick up that report again, I realize how incredibly grateful I was to my highly expert assessors: Dr M. Grunhut MA, Reader in Criminology, University of Oxford; Mr Frank Milton, Magistrate, North London Magistrates' Court; Dr Stafford-Clark, York Clinic, Guy's Hospital, London; and Dr Trevor Gibbens, MD, DPH, Institute of Psychiatry, Maudsley Hospital, Denmark Hill, London. They were, according to an announcement, intended to 'correct any bias' of mine, presumably a bias in a religious direction. Be that as it may, I could truthfully write of them: 'Apart from their other formidable credentials, they must have been deemed between them to have read all that was most relevant to the criminological literature of this and other countries.'

We interviewed every kind of expert. The two witnesses who come most vividly to mind were already well known and destined to become more so: Dr John Bowlby ('Bogey' to me and his other friends), the child psychiatrist, and Professor Barbara Wootton, whom I was later to help introduce to the House of Lords as Baroness Wootton of Abinger. John Bowlby was famous for his theory of maternal deprivation. He insisted that lack of mother love and lack of security in the earliest days was responsible for a large part of criminality. Barbara Wootton had a good deal to say about 'the criminal subculture likely to be associated with poverty'. But when she was asked what help the criminologist could give to the Home Secretary of the day about the causes of crime, she replied 'not much'. Indeed she was to carry her negative influence on the theoretical plane still further in a classic work published in 1959, *Social Science and Social Pathology*. In the history of criminology, she is held to have gone a long way to debunk psychological theories of crime.

It is right, however, to record the considered verdict of Lord Windlesham, former Home Office minister and later Chairman of the Parole Board. In his book *Responses to Crime* (1987), he wrote in connection with alternatives to imprisonment: 'Few penal innovations owe more to a single voice and personality than community service orders owe to Baroness Wootton of Abinger.'

When I myself came to assess the evidence my Nuffield inquiry obtained, I was compelled to adopt a tone of extreme caution in an attempt to conform with scientific requirements. There was general agreement that the idea of a single cause of crime was discredited. There was a general disposition to concur with the doctrine of multiple causation enunciated by Dr Cyril Burt as long ago as 1925. I felt able, however, to stress what seemed the largest single factor. 'There is no doubt,' I wrote, 'that the psychological and moral influence of the family – especially as exercised during the first few years – has become far the most fashionable category among those who write and talk about the causes of crime.' I singled out the broken home as the largest single factor.

It should be mentioned that thirty years ago it was still possible to talk of the 'alleged' increase in crime. According to the official figures, taking 1938 as 100, the figure for 1948 had reached 185. It had come down to 153 in 1954, then started moving upwards to attain 169 in 1956.

When I came to write my final chapter, I pulled myself together. Surely I had some message to impart after such a strenuous investigation and so much expert assistance? I boldly entitled this last chapter 'A New Approach to Crime'.

I was much preoccupied with the question of how far modern theories of psychology left room for free will and therefore moral responsibility and blameworthiness. I concluded that these fundamental concepts were not disturbed, but it was more than ever obvious that human justice was never likely to approximate to Divine justice. 'It obviously becomes more and more difficult to believe in human justice,' I wrote, 'to approve, if you like, the sentences that are passed on human delinquents as we become more and more certain that God is passing very different sentences on them and the rest of us; as it becomes less and less likely that precisely the right people are in prison.'

I drew the interesting practical conclusion: 'So long as we were fairly well satisfied that prisoners were evil-doers who were, roughly speaking, getting what they deserved, we were ready to treat the efforts spent on their reform as an act of social quixotry, a kind of bonus to which they possessed no moral claim. And as a result, the share of our social effort, materially or spiritually speaking, which we have devoted to prisoners, has been pitifully small.'

In other words, my earnest study of the causes of crime had not produced a solution to that problem, or made a solution seem likely. But it had inspired me with a lifelong devotion to the cause of penal reform.

Between the completion of my inquiry (1953) and the publication of the book (1958), I had taken two initiatives of which I am still admittedly proud. In 1955 I had opened the first debate ever held in the House of Lords on prisons. I have spoken repeatedly on that subject since, sometimes initiating the debates. In the same year, and with generous help from others, I had established the New Bridge for Ex-Prisoners, which much assisted by the chairmanship of my friend Lady Ewart-Biggs, now retired, still expands and flourishes.

In 1961, I published a small book called *The Idea of Punishment*. I stressed the traditional elements in a just sentence – deterrence, reform, prevention and retribution – though I suggested that fairness would be a better name for the last-mentioned. I expressed the hope, since then to a small extent fulfilled, that reparation should figure much more prominently in future. I did not attempt to deal with mental offenders, though by that time I was well aware of that far-reaching issue (see page 168). More strangely, I left out all reference to public opinion. Such an omission would be inconceivable today when the remorseless increase in crime has produced such a strong reaction against prisoners in the public mind.

Through my public association with prisoners I was beginning to be asked, 'Why don't you do something for the victims of crime?' I was not slow to bestir myself. The year 1964 was an important one for me in several ways. I was Chairman of a committee of the lawyers' society, Justice, on compensation for victims of violent crime. In fact, I initiated the first debate for many years on that subject in the House of Lords. It was perhaps hardly a coincidence that the first official scheme of compensation for victims of violence was introduced in 1964.

By that time I was being referred to publicly as 'that prison person'. In *Five Lives*, an autobiography published that year, I indeed adopted that title for a substantial section of the book. In that same book I described some of my efforts to help individual prisoners and ex-prisoners. They included the famous Soviet spy George Blake, then serving forty-two years but who subsequently escaped. There is something ironic about my final sentence regarding George Blake: 'I trust that I may be of some slight service to him later.'

To me, the chapter of the book which still seems to be worth reading is entitled 'The Sinner and the Sin', which for many years has summed up my approach to criminals and many others. I was obviously very conscious of the close relationship *in practice* between my Christian approach and that of a supreme Humanist like Barbara Wootton. 'Barbara Wootton and I have disagreed on many points of theory, as a Humanist and a Catholic must. But we have very seldom disagreed, in practice, on anything which concerned the treatment of the convicted or, for that matter, of other unfortunates and deviants. I have sat in her court and admired not only her endless patience and kindness, but her clear association of what I will call impeccable "Christian morality".'

In that same year, 1964, was published a report called *Crime – A Challenge to Us All*, the work of a Labour Party study group set up by Harold Wilson, by that time Leader of the Opposition. I was honoured to be Chairman and still more pleased later when most of our conclusions were put into operation by the subsequent Labour government. In his important report on parole, *The Parole System in England and Wales* (1988), Lord Carlisle of Bucklow was kind enough to single out our committee as the first to recommend a parole system. I could not claim that the idea started with me, though I embraced it then and later with much enthusiasm. We also recommended *inter alia* the abolition of capital punishment, which duly came to pass. But that was already favoured by almost everyone in the Labour Party and by many outside.

When the Labour government was formed in 1964, I entered the Cabinet as Leader of the House of Lords. I was probably the socialist most closely associated with penal reform at the time, but a putative Home Secretary could never be a member of the House of Lords. Evelyn Waugh may or may not have expressed a widespread opinion when he wrote to Frankie (Lady) Donaldson, both of them being my friends: 'I'm glad that Frank is not going to the Home Office. We should all have been murdered in our beds.'

In my Cabinet years (1964 to 1968) I did not make much of a contribution to penal policy, though as Leader of the House of Lords I warmly endorsed the reform measures of the period. One of the few things I am ashamed of in my public life (perhaps I should be ashamed of more) was my failure to go to the wedding of Christopher Craig who had been convicted of murder some years before, but was now making good outside prison. I had come to know him well while he was 'inside'.

The circumstances were somewhat peculiar. Harold Wilson, the Prime Minister, was being harassed by a Tory MP who claimed that I had been using undue influence on behalf of Christopher's brother, Niven, in prison at the time. Indeed, he had gone further and suggested a homosexual relationship. Harold Wilson, head of a government with a highly precarious majority, begged me not to go to Christopher's wedding. I agreed – weakly as I now think. I salved my conscience by giving Christopher and his fiancée dinner the night before the wedding. But that was a feeble compensation.

In 1968 I resigned from the Labour Cabinet because of their failure to keep a recent promise and raise the school-leaving age (it was raised later). I was already committed to a far-reaching inquiry into the treatment of the young. As I could not help the young people from inside the government, I was determined to try to keep faith with them outside. With much invaluable assistance, including that of Jack Profumo, whose great work at Toynbee Hall was getting under way, I started the New Horizon Youth Centre in London.

I had originally thought of New Horizon as a centre for young delinquents, but I was soon convinced that young people of all kinds who needed help should be admitted. Many of our 'visitors' have usually had trouble with the law. Today, it offers friendship and practical help to 3000 or so homeless young people a year, including a good proportion of girls and young blacks. The Chairman is Jon Snow, a Director of the Centre since its early days who has never lost his interest in it as he has gone on to greatness in television.

In the last twenty years, the approach I recommended at the end of *Causes of Crime* in 1958 has had a rough time. The enormous expansion of criminological studies must be welcomed in itself, if we take a long view. It has already helped to destroy the belief that longer sentences are a more effective deterrent than shorter ones. But criminologists have, on the whole, cast serious doubts on the possibility of reparation in prison. And always there has been the relentless increase in crime, with a growing public fear of the criminal, easily exploited and stirred into hatred by the tabloid press.

In recent years much has been written and said, and a small amount has been done, about alternatives to prison. The way is open in the next decade for a great leap forward. Personally I am glad that the present government has boldly faced the issue of punishment in the community, at any rate on paper. I have already mentioned the White Paper *Crime, Justice and Protecting the Public*; to that I must add the Green Paper *Supervision and Punishment in the Community* (1990). I can only hope that the Probation Service, for whom my admiration is unbounded, will be ready to play the part they could play uniquely well.

At the moment of writing, there are more people in prison in Britain per head of the population than in any other European country. The average length of a custodial sentence has increased by 30 per cent in the last few years. It can be taken for granted that to the best of my ability I shall go on struggling against such developments and in favour of the utmost use of alternative remedies in which the convicted persons will work for the benefit of the community.

I will round off these recollections with a reference to two prisoners with whose names I am now indelibly associated: Ian Brady and Myra Hindley. They were convicted for the appalling Moors murders in 1965 and have confessed to two other murders since. Ian Brady, after twenty years in prison, is now in Ashworth hospital, Liverpool, where the doctors agree he should have been from the beginning. Myra Hindley, his infatuated accomplice, has been in Cookham Wood prison for the last six years. More than twenty years ago I began to visit them both, though it is many years since they were in touch with each other.

Ian Brady does not expect or wish to be released. Myra Hindley was recommended in 1985 for parole by Cookham Wood's local review committee, including the Governor of the prison. She was congratulated by the Chairman of the Committee on her life in prison, including her Open University degree. The Parole Board, acting under I know not what pressures, not only turned down the application for parole but said that it could not be reconsidered for another five years. No one supposes for a moment that Myra Hindley is still dangerous. She is now a deeply religious woman, much liked (to take only three examples) by myself, David Astor, who was Editor of *The Observer* for twenty-seven years, Peter Timms, a former Governor of Maidstone prison and now a

Methodist minister, and by all three of our wives.

In 1990, Myra Hindley became eligible for parole once more and again she was turned down with a recommendation that her application should not be reconsidered for another five years. If I am thinking about justice in connection with prisoners, I take Myra Hindley's continued incarceration as a glaring example of injustice. But Myra is only one of so many of whom this is true. And never for a moment in passing such a judgement should one forget the victims. I will end by recalling the fact that in 1978 I initiated an inquiry into the treatment of victims and in 1979 introduced a Private Member's Bill into the House of Lords for their benefit. My bill had a friendly reception, although it never reached the Statute book. It is terribly hard to remember criminals and their victims in the same perspective, but no Christian can ever fail to make the effort.

I

Administrators of Justice

Lord Windlesham

Lord Windlesham is uniquely equipped as a penal administrator and policy-maker. He was a Conservative Minister of State at the Home Office from 1970 to 1972, from where he went as a Minister of State to Northern Ireland. He was Lord Privy Seal and Leader of the House of Lords from 1973 to 1974 and the Chairman of the Parole Board from 1982 to 1988. There have been many Ministers of State at the Home Office and, for that matter, many Home Secretaries; there have been very few Chairmen of the Parole Board (a fairly new phenomenon). Two at least of them (Lord Harris of Greenwich and Lord Colville of Culross) have also been Ministers of State at the Home Office. But none of these eminent persons has ever written a book like *Responses to Crime*, a comprehensive and first-class account of the penal system. That achievement places Lord Windlesham on a pedestal all his own. I should add that he became Leader of the House of Lords at the age of only forty-one, the youngest in my recollection. He is now Principal of Brasenose College, Oxford.

I have known David Windlesham for a good many years in the House of Lords and had plenty of occasions to admire his speeches and his writings. Naturally in preparing this book I concentrated on *Responses to Crime*, but I also interviewed him at length.

During our meeting, I asked him whether he would regard himself as a defender of the penal system. He replied that he was more interested in describing the workings of the penal system than defending them. There he is certainly on strong ground, for no one with his experience has described it so well.

There is much emphasis in his book on public opinion. Indeed, the first chapter is entitled 'The Setting: Within the Toleration of Public Opinion'. I asked whether he approved of the existing system, subject to desirable reforms; whether on its intrinsic merits it was the best system possible in view of public opinion. 'Public opinion,' he replied, 'sets the limits on what is possible, certainly in terms of ministers who have to carry Parliament and the wider public with them. Penal reformers and special interest groups should never be inhibited by factors of that sort, but ministers are.' Ministers should not, however, simply content themselves with reflecting public opinion, he went on, they should also seek to mould it. A good example was set by Douglas Hurd, until recently Home Secretary, and John Patten, Minister of State at the Home Office, in the way they prepared the ground for the concept of punishment being served in the community instead of in custody. The Probation Service also had to be coaxed in this direction.

I asked him whether he was happy that retribution now seemed to be playing a much larger part in sentencing policy than the attempts at moral reform of twenty years ago. Lord Windlesham seemed uncomfortable about putting it like that. 'I would not be happy to see retribution displacing all thoughts of rehabilitation and reform. They should ride hand in hand, and I would be sorry if the attempt to point the way towards a better way of life for offenders who have been punished were to be abandoned. But it is true that the current is running strongly towards retribution at the moment.'

'Why,' I asked him, 'do you consider that retribution has come to the fore?' 'People are more pessimistic about the efficacy of penal policy. Too great an emphasis on retribution can distort sentencing. The idea of retribution seen as "just deserts" has been imported from the United States. I do not think it has worked out as intended there. Ideals which sounded all right when they were being debated simply have not been borne out in practice, largely because the idea of perfect retribution is unattainable in a democratic political society.'

'If you were Home Secretary with a free hand what, if any, reforms would you introduce?' I continued.

'I would give effect to the Carlisle Report on Parole and the Nathan Report on Murder and Life Imprisonment,' Lord Windlesham replied. Those issues are dealt with below (see pages 163–166 and 166–168).

Lord Windlesham also said that he would take strong initiatives in two particular directions. He is much concerned about the alienation of victims of crime from the administration of justice.

He would take steps to integrate victims and witnesses more closely with court proceedings.

What was more of a surprise to me was his almost passionate desire to separate remand prisoners from convicted prisoners. He set out his views at some length in the March 1988 issue of the *Criminal Law Review*. I fully share his disgust at the long-standing failure to improve the situation of remand prisoners. Thirty years ago, Lord Stonham, a leading penal reformer, referred to Brixton in the House of Lords as the 'hell-hole of Brixton'. That 'hell-hole' is the leading remand prison and it is still there.

I cannot refrain from one reference to the treatment of Myra Hindley by the Parole Board while Lord Windlesham was its Chairman, when the Board turned down her application. Lord Windlesham told me that the Parole Board had always avoided commenting on individual cases, but claimed that Myra Hindley had been considered in a way that was consistent with the policies then in force for the review of life sentence prisoners.

I cannot accept that defence. The policies then in force have few defenders today. And if those policies justified anything, they would justify Myra Hindley being refused parole until she had served twenty years, certainly not until she had served twenty-five or more. Lord Windlesham is a highly intelligent man of honour, but even intelligent and honourable ministers occasionally find themselves in a completely impossible position.

Lord Hunt of Llanfair Waterdine

Lord Hunt of Llanfair Waterdine will go down in history as the leader of the first team to climb Mount Everest. It was typical of him that he sent on two of his team, one of them Edmund Hillary, to attain the summit. Mountaineering has been one of the major inspirations of his life – even the 'dangling airily down some rock wall at the end of an abseil rope'. But even more so has the whole conception of moral leadership. For John Hunt, the leader's place is 'not in front, but in the middle'.

The story I like best of him describes his reaction when asked by the Queen's secretary whether he would agree to become a Knight of the Garter. 'This can't be meant for me,' said John Hunt, and he attempted to send the letter on to another Lord Hunt. But like Clem Attlee, his genuine diffidence conceals a will of iron.

His experience on Everest in 1953 led him to abandon a career in the Army which might have led him to the supreme heights. He had passed first into and out of Sandhurst. Instead, work in the service of youth claimed him and has never relaxed its grip. From 1956 to 1966 he was the first Director of the Duke of Edinburgh's Award Scheme for young people. From 1967 to 1974 he was the first Chairman of the Parole Board. From 1980 to 1985 he was Chairman of the Intermediate Treatment Fund which supported many valid schemes for helping young people aged fourteen to seventeen to find a form of self-expression other than crime. At the end of his chairmanship he wrote: 'The main challenge is to voluntary bodies and to individual people in all walks of life to help the young generation take their place in the community as responsible citizens, and to find satisfaction in their lives.'

I asked Lord Hunt at the beginning of our interview whether his chairmanship of the Parole Board brought him into touch with crime for the first time. 'No,' he replied. In the 1930s, when he was a young officer in Bengal, he was called on to cope with active terrorism. He learned then a lesson which he never forgot. 'I found that a politically active character could often be transformed simply by giving him responsibility. While it lasted it was, for me, a thrilling experience to watch the enthusiasm of boys being channelled into activities more appropriate to their age and circumstances than the study of seditious books, the making of bombs and the plotting of murders.'

I have never heard John Hunt use the expression 'I believe in youth', but it would describe his attitude with regard to the young whether in Bengal or in the inner cities of Britain. He has always believed in their unlimited possibilities given leadership, discipline and opportunity, and he has had the chance to put his beliefs into practice.

'One of my bedside books,' he told me, 'is *Joie de Croire, Joie de Vivre* by a French monk, François Varillon. He wrote in moving terms about the source and power of love. It is certainly my experience of meeting and observing some of those who are engaged in work among young people, that their authority stems from the quality of their caring about the youngsters as individuals, no matter how difficult, alienated and delinquent they may be. This power does not derive from sanctions as a means of exercising control; it is a quality of loving which evokes similar feelings in young people themselves. It is a positive and constructive power, which gives to youth the will to make something of their own lives. It is a power which instils a caring in the young about the needs of others.'

Naturally I pressed Lord Hunt about parole. He has himself done much to establish the scheme within the penal system and to give it credibility during his term as Chairman of the Parole Board. Broadly speaking, he has supported the development of parole though he was not happy, he said, about the refusal to give reasons when parole is refused. Until now, he felt that the administrative difficulties involved would have been too great in view of the very large number of applications.

The greatest merit of the recent Carlisle Report on parole in his opinion is that in future prisoners sentenced to four years or less will be released under supervision automatically when they have completed one-half of their sentence, subject to any extra days added for specific prison misconduct. Thus fewer offenders, only those serving more serious sentences of four years or more, would be screened and selected or refused by the Parole Board. The reduced numbers eligible for parole, he considers, should mean that the Parole Board will be able to give reasons for refusal in individual cases.

I put it to him that the Carlisle Report would actually increase the numbers in prison, except on the unreal hypothesis that the judiciary would much reduce sentences. Like other penal reformers, he fully agrees that such a major reduction in sentences is essential to real progress in penal reform. Moreover, like other penal reformers, he is by no means clear as to how this is to be achieved. He believes that a change in public attitude towards methods of punishment is a necessary precondition. He is ready to give favourable consideration to the idea of a Sentencing Council.

One difference between us emerged, apart from our respective attitudes to the Carlisle Report. In John Hunt's view the main grounds for granting parole are the prospect that, with supervision and support from the Probation Service, the prisoner is less likely to re-offend during the period of his licence than would be the case if he were to complete his sentence in custody. Relevant to this prospect are such factors as accommodation, family circumstances and the prospects of a job. This way of looking at things in my eyes favours unfairly the man with a good home to go back to, against the man with a bad one or no home at all. On this point we had to agree to differ.

This led on to a discussion of punishment. How far does John Hunt agree with the challenging idea of punishment within the community, as set out in the various recent government documents? He of course agrees with anything that would transfer people, particularly young people, from prisons to life in the community. He is positive that young offenders at a formative stage in their lives can more easily become good citizens if the penal treatment they experience is constructive. Long sentences in adult prisons only encourage the young to become professional criminals. But he also agrees in principle with the need for an element of punishment in the treatment of young offenders. In most cases of juvenile delinquency, however, he maintains that 'punishment' should be implicit rather than explicit in supervision orders decreed by the juvenile courts.

As a former President of the National Association of Probation Officers, Lord Hunt is well aware how allergic they are to the very mention of punishment. He considers that the government under-rates the work of the Probation Service, both in regard to their social skills and their exercise of control over young offenders. Both he and I agree that the government would be gravely mistaken if, by requiring the Probation Service to resume its punitive role, they impaired the vital relationship between officers and offenders.

Judge Stephen Tumim

Judge Stephen Tumim is Her Majesty's Chief Inspector of Prisons and a man of much potential significance in the penal world. A friendly profile in *The Observer* said of him: 'With the spotted bow tie and half-moon specs, he has the kindly quizzical manner of one of the Cheeryble brothers.' His obvious sense of humour conceals an audacious, even iconoclastic spirit. He is a man of culture, the Chairman of the Friends of the Tate; his three daughters are talented artists and designers. His wife stood as an Alliance candidate in 1983 and 1987 – another indication of boldness.

He was a county court judge for seven years, some anxiety about his health, it seems, preventing his taking silk. I have no means of knowing why Douglas Hurd, then Home Secretary, appointed him Chief Inspector of Prisons, but it has proved an inspired choice.

Judge Tumim's annual report of 1988 is a depressing document, although intensely readable. There are good points to the prison system, he maintains, but his general conclusions are condemnatory.

> Local prisons remain generally overcrowded, insanitary and offering little use for activities for inmates. . . . We were concerned at the lack of uniform provision in many areas which are key to the humanity and dignity of prisoners' lives. . . . There is no guarantee that all inmates will be properly and correctly treated in these important areas.

Possibly in accordance with protocol, he lays the responsibility throughout his report on the Prison Department. We political persons are surely correct in blaming ministers, whatever their party.

I was pleasantly surprised at the role which Judge Tumim seems to have assumed with official approval of bringing together judges and prison governors. The relationship has hitherto been exiguous. He himself has seen more of the inside of prisons than any judge has ever seen, but in general the Prison Service still feels ignored by the judges, and rightly so. Speaking as a judge to other judges, Stephen Tumim is trying to 'build the judges into the system' as in other countries in Europe and in the United States. The importance of this cannot be overestimated, for Judge Tumin has set himself no less a task than that of attempting to promote a coherent criminal justice system. If he succeeds even partially, the effect on sentencing policy could be profound.

I asked Judge Tumim whether prisons could be much improved with the existing prison population, or only if it were very much reduced. 'We ask,' he replied, 'the wrong questions about imprisonment in England. We keep asking: Should we be nicer or should we be nastier to prisoners? This ends up in discussing punishment, just deserts, which are really names for vengeance.'

As Chief Inspector of Prisons, Judge Tumim asks: Does the regime train for life outside? Is this prison a pre-release course in itself? To him, training is the most important thing. 'Too much work in prison is dull and repetitious,' he believes. 'That sort of work is not training. It is defended by the authorities as "work experience", but it is of no value if dull and off-putting. There should be more qualifications and down-to-earth training. At present far too much is posed on an assumption that nothing will work.'

The young? 'It is unfortunate that we do not use trained youth workers. Young people are left to prison staff who are used to looking after old lags. There should be specialized youth workers and more women officers working with young men.' Judge Tumim is making a study of how prisoners pass their time from morning till night – how long in education, slopping out and so on.

Concerning occupation and training, Judge Tumim believes that there are far too many prisoners left in their cells with nothing to do. When visiting a prisoner, he came across some Kurds who did not speak English. When he reported this, he was told: 'We don't teach English as a foreign language here.' He also believes that rehabilitation is the wrong word to use of prisoners, when some have never even been 'habilitated' to begin with. Prison should be a pre-release course. 'Prison should be a preparation for going back into the community; 55 per cent of men are reconvicted within two years of release, and 75 per cent of teenagers.'

It must not be thought that Judge Tumim is a woolly-minded idealist, his eyes fixed on a far-distant future. He lays almost obsessive emphasis on the improvement of sanitary conditions, for example. He sees this as the first step to making life in prison not only sanitary but sane. Disraeli said in the 1870s that the policy of the Conservative Party was *sanitas sanitatum omnia sanitas*. Judge Tumim might adopt that as his motto. But in all sorts of other ways he insists that physical improvements could open up new possibilities of moral growth in prisons.

'What,' I asked him, 'is the argument for retaining prisons if training is to be our sole main objective?' He replied that many of those at present sent to prison could be trained more economically outside prison. There should be much more effective community service orders. He stressed that a number of people would always have to be locked up for public security. He laid the utmost stress on not locking up so many remand prisoners. Again and again, Judge Tumim returned to prison as being a training for life afterwards. Probation officers should be job-finders and helpers in occupation and training when a prisoner comes out on licence (parole). He welcomed the recommendations in *Crime, Justice and Protecting the Public* for supervision on licence by probation officers. 'Prisons should train. Probation officers should find jobs.'

I asked him to make sure I understood his meaning as to whether any room should be left for punishment. 'Training is the aim; punishment may be part of it. I am not suggesting that training should be soft.' Let me quote from Judge Tumim's annual report for 1989, which alas gives no more grounds for optimism in its general conclusions than his report for 1988.

We need to concentrate on occupation and education, and, pre-eminently on training. It is necessary but not sufficient to have prisons which securely contain. Training and dispersal prisons must train for 'after release'. Local and remand centres must be relieved of insanitary squalor and overcrowding and must offer short-term training, including work qualifications. Young Offender Institutions must show a genuine advance on prisons in the training they produce: it is often the very last chance for the inmate. . . .

The reduction of stress must be another element in successful training. Long before the 1990 disturbances, prison officers suffered from working in a stressful atmosphere. We comment quite sharply in this report on defects we have noticed in medical services for inmates; we observe also the omissions in support services for prison staff. The stress of many prisoners could be lowered without much expense in a number of ways. . . .

In 1990 we have already run into a series of events, ranging from the grossest riots by prisoners to the reorganization of the senior part of the prison service, and to industrial unrest and dissatisfaction with some of the consequences of Fresh Start. . . . However dramatic and newsworthy these and further events and reports may prove to be, we must hope that the sensible priority of greatly improved training will not get lost.

It will be understood by now why I call Judge Tumim 'audacious, even iconoclastic'. If his ideas were applied on a large scale, the whole of our prison system would look totally different. What is so marvellous is that this revolutionary idealist should be saying the things which penal reformers have said for many years, and has obtained a position by dint of his personality where those in power have to listen to him. It is good news indeed that Judge Tumim is sharing the responsibility for the report on Strangeways and the underlying issues which Lord Justice Woolf was asked to undertake.

Lord Allen of Abbeydale

Lord Allen of Abbeydale was Permanent Under-Secretary of State at the Home Office from 1966 to 1972. He was Assistant Under-Secretary there from 1952 to 1955 and Deputy Under-Secretary from 1960 to 1962, although his distinguished career as a civil servant included many other postings. He first entered the Home Office in 1934.

Lord Longford: You have an unrivalled experience of prison administration.

Lord Allen: I joined the Home Office straight from Cambridge in 1934 and was put in the Criminal Division. One of my main responsibilities there was advising on the prerogative of mercy. In fact I began my official career by looking at the mistakes the courts had made.

LL: You had to prevent people being hanged?

LA: No, I am talking of the ordinary run of cases. I can give you one example of a prisoner who got eight years; he had a long list of convictions for sending letters demanding money with menaces. Unfortunately, after he had been sent to prison the letters continued to arrive. In the end it was clear that he should never have been convicted, and we had to give him a free pardon. This happened in my first few months. It has left me ever since with a slight doubt in my mind about the functioning of the courts and whether they invariably reach the right answer.

Much later in my career, I was involved in the case of Timothy Evans. An inquiry by a judge reached the conclusion that he probably did not commit the murder for which he had been executed. At the very least had it been known about Christie, Evans would never have been hanged.

LL: Was someone clearly in error?

LA: I don't think we shall ever know the full circum-
        stances. I am no lawyer, but I have been for one
        reason or another much concerned with trying to
        improve the functioning of the courts. My first visit to
        the House of Commons was in connection with the
        Criminal Justice Bill before the war.

LL: Was that Samuel Hoare's?

LA: Yes, he was then Home Secretary. His Bill was
        revived again after the war. I have been concerned
        with a few Criminal Justice Bills ever since.

LL: What is the result of all that? Do you think you have
        some special angle?

LA: I think throughout one has been pursuing this aim –
        to ensure that only those who are sent to prison really
        deserve to be. We saw, when I first started, that there
        was a great number of people in prison in default of
        payment of debt – there still are. A great number of
        people were being sent to prison for very short
        periods, which seemed to me to serve no very good
        purpose. They just had time enough to get ac-
        quainted with general criminals and out they came.

        There were three points which struck me: first, the
        ability of the courts to make mistakes; second, the
        sending of too many people to prison; and then there
        was the great disparity of sentences. One repeatedly
        discovered on visiting prisons that very few judges
        had ever been there. I was struck by the ignorance of
        the judiciary as to what they were sending people to.

        When we started sentencing conferences – it must
        have been in the sixties but I am leaping ahead – one
        of the great problems I found as Permanent Under-
        Secretary was keeping in touch with the judges.

LL: Judge Tumim, the Chief Inspector of Prisons, sees
        himself as a liaison officer – the contact between the
        Home Office and the judiciary.

LA: Such contact hardly existed in my earlier days and the valiant efforts we made were really not at all successful. I did make some progress with Parker when he was Lord Chief Justice, but not with Widgery. There was a speech in one debate about the splendid training of the judges – but in practice it was not quite like that at all. One of the things that struck me right at the beginning was the disparity of the sentences – some of them absolutely lenient and certainly not too severe.

I kept returning to the Home Office and have been dealing either with crime or with gaols or, as Under-Secretary, with both. Two of the great changes I have seen during my time have been the abolition of corporal punishment and capital punishment. It was often said by some of the right-wingers that when a man has had the cat-o'-nine-tails he would never offend again. When I was a Prison Commissioner and a man came up for a second or third time – what do you do?

LL: Would it be true to say that you played a part in the abolition of either of these?

LA: Yes, a humble back-room part. I don't mind saying that I was advising on capital punishment. I did become a confirmed abolitionist. I often wondered, when I was Permanent Under-Secretary, what I would have done if the Home Secretary of the day had decided to reintroduce capital punishment to which I felt such a moral aversion.

LL: Looking back, would you agree that on the whole life in prison today is rather worse than it was thirty years ago?

LA: I think it is, partly because of increased external standards. Generally it seems worse – standards outside have gone up and so has overcrowding in very old buildings. What tends to be forgotten is that when we made demands to get money either for new prisons or for the rehabilitation of the old ones, it was very expensive. You are providing for people twenty-four hours a day, seven days a week, with high security. In the post-war years what hope had we got in persuading the Cabinet and the public that enormous resources should be spent on cosseting criminals rather than on roads, schools, houses and all the rest of the things that more deserving members of the community were calling for? We had terrible battles in Cabinet to get more money.

The present government talk as though nothing ever happened until they took office. We did create twenty-six new penal establishments of one kind or another, six of them high-security prisons, between 1958 and 1979. The latter provided something like 8000 places. That all seems to me to be forgotten. We had a particular scheme approved by the Home Secretary which was kiboshed when the IMF were called in and economies were rife all round.

LL: On a crude level, Judge Tumim told me that Mrs Thatcher is keen on better sanitation. After all these years, one feels it has been the reluctance of ministers and the public that prevented the Home Office getting enough money for prisons. Have Home Office officials always *wanted* to obtain more?

LA: We all recognized how hopeless it was. Whether it ought to have been pressed harder – I don't know.

LL: Peter Timms – who went into prison service at an early age and was Governor of Maidstone – says that more time is now spent in the cells. What appals me about this is that they say the ratio of prison officers to prisoners is much higher than when he joined the service. Is this due to restrictive practices on the part of prison officers? There is said to be a shortage of prison officers and yet the ratio now is so much higher.

LA: It is not so much to do with how long prisoners are in
        their cells, but with what they do when they are out of
        them. One of the problems is the inability to develop
        the educational side. You don't need prison officers
        but teachers for that. More importantly, you have to
        find work that prisoners can do, and what the trade
        unions will allow them to do without saying that their
        workers are being undercut. I think the conditions
        are worse, but that is a direct result of the increased
        numbers of prisoners. It is easier to employ ten
        thousand than fifty thousand.

LL: Coming now to the immediate present – you, like
        myself, are quite sympathetic to punishment in the
        community?

LA: Yes, but if you go too far in that direction you will
        never persuade the courts or the public that it really
        is punishment, and not just a soft option.

LL: It is difficult to carry the Probation Service with you
        – and the judges.

LA: I think the Probation Service have got their heads too
        far in the clouds.

LL: We both agree that community service is a good idea
        in the abstract. Are there things which you would
        particularly like to emphasize?

LA: I would like something to be said about the efforts
        which have been made over the years. The im-
        pression has been given that governments over the
        years have sat back and done very little, but there has
        been a great deal of experimentation. We have intro-
        duced parole, suspended sentences, majority
        verdicts and detention centres. We have flirted with
        corrective training and preventive detention. These
        were all experiments – some succeeded, some did
        not. The last two did not, but the fact that corrective

training failed was not our fault – unfortunately, the judges failed to understand it.

LL: And then, of course, the abolition of corporal and capital punishment. But this must have come from outside the Home Office?

LA: It depends on the Home Secretary of the day.

LL: But in the Home Office of the day there must have been a wish for it to go?

LA: I am the only Permanent Under-Secretary of the Home Office to come to the Lords, other than those in the Treasury, the Foreign Office or the Cabinet Office. [Lord Allen was implying, I think, that the standing of the Home Office in Whitehall is not as great as is often supposed.]

LL: Do you feel that any ministers have been constructive in the world of penal treatment?

LA: Lord Butler and Roy Jenkins were well ahead of others.

LL: I thought that RAB made a wonderful beginning. I found a new atmosphere, but he got absorbed in other things.

LA: To be fair, he had a genuine desire for prison reform without any very clear concept himself of what he wanted to achieve.

LL: Do you feel that the findings of the Mountbatten Committee of 1966 led to an undue emphasis on security?

LA: It probably did, but at the time there had been so many escapes, so much had gone wrong that the prison service had begun to lose credibility. There was one particular man, a mad axeman, who got out of Dartmoor and Winchester. The prison service as a whole was at serious risk of losing public confidence and I would emphasize that we did not go as far as Mountbatten recommended.

LL: It is widely said that the rehabilitation model has failed and we have now got to move on to retribution – the new emphasis in the government papers is on 'just deserts'. When I wrote *The Idea of Punishment*, retribution was then thought of as a reactionary thing. It is now back in favour. How do you feel about this new emphasis? It is connected with the idea that rehabilitation has failed. Research has done a lot to discredit it.

LA: Some regard has got to be paid to retribution. I can see the argument that if you have a particularly dangerous offender, it is better for the community that he should be safely locked away. But whether this is the same thing as retribution . . .

LL: The emphasis is on proportionality.

LA: I have considerable doubts about it. I find it terribly difficult to isolate these philosophical attributes. I can see the argument for keeping a dangerous person out of circulation. This is often called prevention. When one comes to consider the release of murderers serving life sentences, it always seems to me to be relevant as to whether the prisoner would be dangerous if he were let out.

I am not too happy about just deserts, but equally I am not too happy about rehabilitation. I know it is still the proclaimed aim to send people out of prison better than when they come in. It is not easy when they spend their lives mixing with other criminals.

LL: Judge Tumim thinks prisons should be places of training.

LA: I don't see how this can be done. Some of the open prisons are more promising.

LL: I am surprised you did not develop them more.

LA: There was always the risk of being discredited if people escaped. I have read a lot of the literature and the theory, but have not got much of a theory myself.

LL: You are a pragmatist . . .

LA: I don't see that as a judge you can say: 'Well, deterrence three years, a just sentence four years, and so on.'

LL: How are you going to persuade judges to pass lighter sentences or send fewer people to prison? What do you think of the sentencing councils now being recommended?

LA: I am not sure how it would operate. The only solution is to get better training for the judges. I know of one or two young judges who have had no training whatsoever. I do regard sentencing conferences as very important. There should be a requirement for the judges to explain their reasons. When we discussed the Carlisle Report in the House of Lords, no judge even bothered to turn up.

LL: Parole is rather in the doghouse, but you have not turned against that?

LA: No, provided it is accompanied by a proper sentencing policy.

LL: Do you favour the reduction of maximum penalties?

LA: Yes, I do, and this has been happening to some extent for certain selected offences, for example burglary.

LL: Is there anything you would like to touch on that I haven't raised?

LA: You have not said anything about Broadmoor. Going back to my earlier days – I was responsible for Broadmoor. There was a triennial review of all the patients and you got the same report over three years

– insane, and so on. So I went to Broadmoor just before the war to see some of these people. We began with a campaign not necessarily of releasing patients but of getting them removed to regular mental hospitals – getting their families interested.

Everything said by Lord Allen was judicious, expert, kindly.

Mary Tuck

Mary Tuck is a married lady with four children and is highly qualified academically. She makes an imposing but kindly impression. I asked her whether there was anything in her qualifications indicating that she was a criminologist. She told me in reply that she had a Master's degree in Social Psychology from the London School of Economics, and other degrees from Oxford. She has worked in many fields besides criminology, but for the last ten years, until her retirement, she had worked at the Home Office Research and Planning Unit. For the last five years she was its Director, responsible for a wide programme of criminological research. Her services in research brought her a CBE. She has established several criminological studies of her own, besides editing other people's work, and given many lectures and papers. Since retiring recently from the Home Office, she had taken up a Fellowship in criminological studies at the Cranfield School of Policy Studies. At the time of writing she is one of Lord Justice Woolf's assessors.

Since I wrote *The Idea of Punishment* in 1961, there has been a tremendous expansion of criminology which had only just begun to be studied in Britain at that time, and at the same time a remorseless increase in crime. Most people would now agree that those in prison are, on average, treated worse than they need to be. 'Can it be said that the study of criminology has led in any way to more enlightened policies?' I asked Mary Tuck. 'Would things be worse if it had not been for criminology? One great improvement in my eyes has been the abolition of capital punishment. But can that be said to owe much to criminology?'

'Policy on capital punishment,' she replied, 'is a good example of how criminology interacts with actual decisions. Criminology was useful in examining all the evidence and testing various rhetorical arguments against fact. Does the death penalty, for instance, really reduce the frequency of murder? There is a mass of criminological evidence on this, much of it summarized recently by Dr Roger Hood of Oxford University for the United

Nations. Criminology was able to show that there is not a great deal of substance in most of the arguments usually made for the death penalty; and, as you know, criminological evidence entered substantially into debatès in Parliament on the issue. But at the end of the day, the decision was for elected legislators, not for criminologists. And that is as it should be. Criminology – which is the scientific study of crime – can test assertions, produce theories, measure empirical realities. But it can't produce our values for us. Society as a whole, not criminologists, decides on our policies about crime.

I asked Mary Tuck about the increase in the volume of crime which made the public more hostile to prisoners. In what sense had criminology been any help to ministers in the last thirty years? 'That is a difficult question, because it is really a lot of questions wrapped into one. You are assuming that there has been a big growth in crime and that this is connected with the fact that prisons are no more civilized places now – indeed possibly less – than they were thirty years ago.'

'Why has criminology not been able to stop the growth in crime, or at least prevent the deterioration in the treatment of prisoners?' I pressed her.

Mary Tuck warned me that it was not 'as clear as all that' that there had been an enormous increase in crime. Criminologists could show that a lot of the growth was in *revealed crime*. We had more policemen, more telephones, more insurance, more computers; hence more crime – especially property crime – was written down and counted these days. She was not saying, she went on, that the amount of crime experienced had not risen at all, but that it had risen less than people thought; and when it had risen, it was often because there was more prosperity, more things to steal. Quite simply, there were more opportunities for crime.

'For instance,' Mary Tuck went on, 'about a quarter of all recorded crime is theft of or from a car. In 1957 there were only 7500 thefts involving motor cars recorded in the whole of England and Wales. By 1987 there were 390,000 such thefts. That number would have accounted for 70 per cent of all the crime recorded in 1867. But you know, as well as I do, that there simply were not many cars about in 1957; nor was it the usual practice to leave these large, valuable, easily broken-into machines untended on the street day and night. More cars means more car-theft – and vehicle-related crime is a quarter of all crime.'

Mary Tuck admitted that criminology has not stopped the amount of recorded crime going up. 'But it has helped us to understand why it is going up, and so has led to the whole crime prevention movement. This is common ground now for all political parties and it has been a research-led movement – indeed led, I would think, from the Home Office Research and Planning Unit. We must never forget that 95 per cent of all crime is property crime and that much of this is preventable by quite simple methods. So one of my answers to your question of how has criminology helped is by pointing to the need for crime prevention and suggesting that these techniques must be a major part of our response to crime.'

I pointed out that she had not yet answered my question as to why the last thirty years had seen a deterioration in the treatment of prisoners. Lord Windlesham had said in *Responses to Crime* that the theory of rehabilitation, the idea that prisons can somehow make people better, is now very much discredited, so why did we see such a heavy use being made of prisons?

'Criminologists,' Mary Tuck replied, 'have often asked that. But once again the interactions of criminology and policy are complex. In the earlier years of this century, there was a sort of Fabian consensus that you could improve people through the criminal justice system; that if only you could find the right way, you could somehow make people better. The old Borstal indeterminate sentence was based on that type of thinking. Boys were not let out until they had received the full "benefit" of the "treatment". Unfortunately, this sort of thing would lead to really long sentences.'

Mary Tuck said that this had been specially marked in America where they went overboard for what was known as 'the treatment model'. Was it not George Jackson of the Soledad Brothers who was kept in prison for decades for the theft of only a few dollars, because the psychiatrists thought he was not improved enough? A lot of work was done by criminologists to see if it was possible to match 'disposals' to offenders, and to provide suitable 'treatment'. But the results were very gloomy. That is where the catch-phrase 'nothing works' came from. The criminologists established that whatever the 'disposal' given to prisoners – long sentences, short sentences, fines, probation, whatever – the rate of re-offending afterwards was pretty similar. So the usual rationales given for long prison sentences were shown by criminologists to be not very sensible.

She had to face the fact that 'prison didn't wither away'. 'The reason,' Mary explained, 'is that prison has become the ideal type of how you deal with offenders. It was not always so. Historians like Foucault show that what they call "the carceral society" – the society which saw prison as the apex and type of how to deal with offenders – was quite a late invention. In this country it had a lot to do with Jeremy Bentham. And despite Bentham the British went on using other forms of disposals, like transportation, until quite late. And we still use fines a lot more than the Americans do. It is America that is still the main "carceral society", imprisoning a vast proportion of its population. And of course their crime rates are the worst of all. They are not a very good advertisement for the effectiveness of prisons. But the work of the criminologists has certainly put a huge question mark over the usefulness of prisons.'

I can recognize the value of that achievement even if, on the base of it, it is negative. I could not help pointing out to Mary, however, 'But the Americans have the most criminology of all and you have said yourself that the Americans use prisons most. Criminology does not seem to have helped them!' Mary Tuck provided an answer: 'Unfortunately, a lot of American criminology seems to me to have focused on finding alternative justifications for prison, once the theory of rehabilitation became doubtful. It is as if they could not imagine any other way of dealing with crime. There has been a lot of work done on what is called in the jargon "incapacitation" – locking people up so that at least they do not commit more crimes while they are inside. It can be shown that most crime is committed by a small minority of offenders who commit crimes very frequently. If you can identify these career criminals or "violent predators" at an early stage and make sure they are locked up for a good long time, then, the theory goes, you will reduce crime rates.'

Mary Tuck continued: 'And you can go quite a long way by good actuarial methods towards identifying at an early stage which young offenders are likely to turn into violent predators, or frequent offenders. So you could get a situation where two fifteen-year-olds have committed very similar crimes: one would be more or less let off, but the other would be locked up for a good long time, because your statistical predictions tell you that he is likely to turn into a frequent offender if left outside.'

I told her that I would regard that as utterly unjust. She agreed with me. 'Especially since most of the statistical predictors turn out to be things like being black, living in the inner city and generally being poor and deprived.' But there is a scientific objection too. 'However successful the statistical predictors, you still get a lot of "false positives" and "false negatives" – that is, you are selecting out some of the wrong people. And what is more, because so many of the crimes that are committed never get into the criminal justice system at all, whatever you do has only a very marginal effect on crime rates. It has been calculated that you would have to *double* the American prison population – already by far the highest in the Western world – to get a 1 per cent reduction in American crime.'

I returned to my submission that we had a very high prison population in this country, living in rather worse circumstances than thirty years ago. How has criminology helped? Mary Tuck went on: 'Well, at least it has peeled away some of the false rationales for prison. And it perhaps leaves more stark why we really put people in prison. We want to punish them.'

Lord   The theory is that if someone has done something
Longford: wrong, they should be punished?

Mary Tuck: Yes, I think that is the real bottom line of why
            society imprisons people. Criminal law is a sort of
            statement of the minimum necessary rules for a
            society. You should not commit murder, fraud,
            rape, whatever, and if you do, there is a sanction.
            That seems to me what criminal law is about.

LL: But there used to be a widespread feeling that if you committed murder, you should be hanged. This is now discredited. Hanging is no unique deterrent. Criminology has helped to discredit deterrence.

MT: You have to be careful about deterrence. You have to distinguish between what criminologists call individual deterrence and general deterrence. Even if it can be shown that a particular punishment does not deter the individual offender, there still remains the function of general deterrence to, as it were, frighten the others. The purpose of the criminal law is to state on behalf of society as a whole that certain behaviours are untenable. That entails punishment.

LL: Thomas Aquinas said it long ago: 'Training that operates by fear of punishment is the kind of training the law imposes.' But even if I agreed with you, why should that punishment be prison?

MT: Well, of course it need not be! It is the whole argument of the recent government White Paper [*Crime, Justice and Protecting the Public*] that all sanctions the courts impose are punishments of varying gradation. Probation orders, community service, fines – they are all punishments, some more severe, some less severe. The trouble is that many in the probation service, and many penal reformers, do not like to think that disposals like probation are in any sense 'punishments'. The whole ethos of the probation service – and there is something magnificent about it – is that they are the offender's 'friend'. They dislike seeing their function as in any way punitive. But that seems to me quite importantly wrong. After all, the probation service do not just go out and befriend anyone. They deal with those who have been assigned to them by due processes of law.

In effect, compulsion is put on the offender to report to the probation officer, despite the element of contract in the relationship. This compulsion can only be justified in a free society as 'punishment'. In a free society, one can't order just anyone to see a probation officer regularly. That is why some concept of 'just deserts', of a punishment to fit the crime, is needed if the rights and liberties of the offender are to be protected.

LL: Are you in favour of 'just deserts'?

MT: I am. In many ways it has been an unpopular concept in criminology in this country, certainly among penal reformers. But I think some sort of concept of justice is necessary as a protection both against the wilder excesses of the 'treatment' model and against the wilder excesses of public opinion. Chesterton argued long ago – against Shaw and the Fabians – that he would far rather be sentenced by a judge than by a psychiatrist, because at least the judicial sentence was not open-ended. The whole history of treatment ideology since his time has shown his wisdom.

LL: I cannot help thinking that human beings are not very good at deciding on 'just deserts'. In practice does it not mean that you are left relying on public opinion? Responsible people should not be unduly swayed by public opinion.

MT: I do not think that specific decisions about individual offenders should depend on public opinion. The law says precisely that this should not happen. Where public opinion has a role is in helping to form some sort of scale of the seriousness of offences. Everyone knows, for instance, that murder is more serious than theft. And people can grade all sorts of offences on some sort of scale. What the scale will not tell you is what sort of *quantum* of punishment should go with a certain seriousness of offence.

Mary Tuck then went on to make a statement which I must record as she made it without my necessarily agreeing: 'So long as the punishment is in the same sort of order as the perceived seriousness of the offence, people do not seem to mind very greatly where you anchor the scales.' When she talks of people, she is speaking internationally. She continued: 'The Dutch, for instance, grade the seriousness of offences in much the same way as we do in this country. But their sentences are roughly half as long for the same level of seriousness. They have much the same crime rates as we do – but a much smaller prison population. It seems a much more sensible way of going about things. There is nothing sacred about the current British levels of sentencing. Indeed, our current tradition of long sentences is not all that old. The Victorians quite often measured prison sentences in days only and gave some very short sentences indeed.'

I turned to the question of parole. I had pointed out in the House of Lords that the Carlisle Report, taking it as it stood, would increase the number of people in prison. What had Mary Tuck to say about that? She generously replied: 'I thought your speech was a good speech. It is perfectly true that you do not accept the Carlisle reforms, unless there is some sort of trade-off with the judiciary. If something much more like the full sentences they impose are necessarily to be served, then they must look more carefully at their own sentencing patterns, and ask themselves if they are not over-using custody.'

I asked Mary whether she agreed with 'so-called enlightened people' that sentences in Britain were too long?

'In my experience,' she said, 'this is totally accepted by anyone who looks seriously at the matter. Certainly international comparisons show it. The great problem in our society is the judiciary. They need to think a great deal more seriously about sentence lengths and about the uses of custody. Roughly one-sixth of the prison population is made up of men sentenced for recidivist burglary. If the judges reduced the mean average sentence for burglary by half, they would transform our prisons at a stroke.

And I do not see why they should not do it. The Dutch and the Germans have shorter sentences for this crime with no ill effects. As I have argued, long sentences neither reduce the amount of burglary committed by any appreciable extent nor help to reform the individual burglars.'

Did she agree with the NACRO (National Association for the Care and Resettlement of Offenders) plan for a Sentencing Council?

Mary Tuck replied that we obviously needed some sort of machinery for more careful, rational consideration of comparative sentence lengths, but it was a matter of 'pragmatic and political possibilities' what form such machinery should take. The wrong Sentencing Council could just make matters worse and a Sentencing Council would only work if it were well-informed. 'The most likely way for reform to come is for the Court of Appeal to have some sort of research staff and to consider sentence lengths seriously across the board for usual as well as unusual offences. In West Germany judges and lawyers have themselves been in the lead in penal reform and see it as part of their function to ensure that citizens are not imprisoned too often and for too long for inadequate reasons. And as a result, the West Germans have both a falling prison population and falling crime rates. I would like to see the British judiciary taking responsibility for our liberties in the same sort of way.'

LL: What about altering the law to facilitate lower sentences? After all, Parliament has final responsibility.

MT: It is very unlikely that you would get reductions in maximum sentences through Parliament.

LL: The official line is that sentences should come down.

MT: But there would always be a temptation in Parliament for individual members – or even parties – to bid up sentence lengths to show they were really tough on crime. It would become a sort of auction of punitiveness. At least that is what I think,

47

though you may tell me that I am cynical about our legislators.

Finally, I asked Mary whether she wanted to say anything about the Christian approach. She thought that a great deal of traditional Christian moral thinking was to be found implicitly, if not overtly, in *Crime, Justice and Protecting the Public*. The Home Office minister, John Patten, who had been especially connected with it, and with whom she had worked personally, was, like herself, a Catholic.

It would be impertinent to try to sum up such authoritative and deeply pondered answers in a few sentences. I was left with the impression that the only way to influence the judiciary in the direction of shorter sentences was to bring to bear on them the results of the best contemporary research. The new concept of punishment in the community as an alternative to punishment in custody itself owes much to research. It may provide the judiciary with the alternatives which, it is to be hoped, they will look to increasingly in the future.

The Revd Peter Timms

The Revd Peter Timms was for many years a leading prison governor, in his case of Maidstone prison. For some years now he has been a Methodist minister, continuing, however, to play a leading role in promoting penal reform. The Butler Awards for the best service rendered within the prison service owe much to his initiative. He has provided personal counselling to Myra Hindley, among many other prisoners. We spoke before the Strangeways riot, at a time when conditions were thought to be improving.

I began by asking what had led him to become a prison officer in the first place.

Peter Timms: My wife and I – we were newly married – prayed for guidance. I was a very young man of twenty-one when I made the decision and it was in response to prayer. I had never seen a prison wall – had no idea what a prison looked like. It must have been a response to some kind of inner awareness of what I should do.

Lord
Longford: Which year was that?

PT: 1951.

LL: Had you ever been moved by the idea of prisons?

PT: I had never given prisons a thought, as far as I was aware.

LL: Looking back, would you say that things are very different in prisons today – better or worse?

PT: I think they are slightly worse. A change is going on at the moment. The prison service in the late 1950s had a vision that reform and change were central – the care of prisoners was central to the nature of the job. In a way, in spite of the enormous problems, the prison service was in the vanguard of changes in social work. The idea of using group counselling and group therapy as a method of developing insight among prisoners was being forged in a number of prisons – Wakefield, for example – long before it gained general acceptance.

LL: When did things begin to fade?

PT: With the advent of the Mountbatten Report in the 1960s, sadly, because for the most part only the punitive aspects of the report were selected.

There was an enormous amount of investment in security – all the paraphernalia of electronic devices and television cameras – and yet Mountbatten had clearly stated for the first time ever that the role of the prison officer should be a welfare and rehabilitative one. This was implicit in what is said in the report and Lord Mountbatten confirmed it to me himself. From that time until recently, almost no money has been spent at all on a crucial part of the prison officer's role – the rehabilitative aspect. The prison task has always been a balance between competing forces of punishment or custody and treatment.

The prison service has experienced its most glorious moments when it has held these things in balance and not believed that one should be subservient to the other. That was demonstrated in 1963 for the first time in history. The Prison Officers' Association went on record at their conference to say that they wanted to commit themselves to a welfare and rehabilitative role for prisons. The Mountbatten Report was used to extend security at the expense of treatment and that was an enormous step backwards – the last thing Mountbatten himself wanted.

LL: Who were the villains who were concentrating on custody?

PT: The real villain was fear of the political process. I think it was a fear – the Prison Department place a very high value on serving the minister, and they have to judge what the minister wants and seek somehow to do that. I am sure they tried desperately not to impose their own views on him. On the contrary, my impression throughout my whole prison service has been that the people within the Prison Department – senior people – have been predominantly people of vision and compassion.

LL: So you believe that the Prison Department, acting from the highest motives, are the people who produce these failures?

PT: I believe it is what the minister wanted. When Shirley Williams was at the Home Office as Minister of State, she was known to say, 'I don't want this, I want that.' The impression within the prison service was that Shirley Williams had an insight into what was needed and was prepared, in fact, to stop the process and reverse things.

I asked Peter Timms whether he was referring to the increased emphasis on security following the Mountbatten Report. He replied that its implementation had led to an imbalance and that imbalance had fed a punitive poison into the system. There is always a temptation on the part of all prison staff to believe in the illusion that the job can be simple if you just concentrate on locking people up. We all look for simple solutions, and yet prison officers know deep within themselves that the job is not like that at all.

PT: When he opens a man's cell in the morning, a prison officer demonstrates what he thinks by the way he says 'good morning' or indeed 'good night'. He reflects his interpretation of the nature of the work he is doing. What happens is 'good morning', 'good morning', and so on down the line. That is the heart of the prison system. But if you say to that officer 'The real objective is locking the door, not saying "good night" – if you say that, you put a punitive tension into the system.

LL: How would you begin to introduce a different attitude?

PT: Interestingly enough, it happens by default, because human beings are fundamentally good. In other words, being bad, evil and nasty is an aberration of what we are meant to be. In spite of the diabolical situation they face in prison, officers still do creative work which flies in the face of the absence of resources.

    Take exhortation. It is always going to be an uphill struggle to get rid of the dustbins in society and we have to recognize that. But let me say very clearly that, for the first time, the Prison Department now displays in every prison waiting-room and meeting room, a beautiful coloured plaque which says:

    Her Majesty's Prison Service serves the public by keeping in custody those committed by the courts. Our duty is to look after them with humanity and to help them lead law-abiding and useful lives in custody and after release.

That is what prison is about. It is a very important statement from the Director-General. I wrote to him and said: 'This is the most important thing you have ever done, but please make sure that in three years' time you change the colour!' When I now visit prisons, I always look for those plaques. It is an important interpretation of the original rules. The essence of it is that we should treat people with dignity.

LL: Was it the Director-General's idea or a previous minister's? John Patten is credited with this view – *vide* the White Paper, *Crime, Justice and Protecting the Public*.

PT: It is the resurgence of the rehabilitative ideal. In the prison system you need to keep your eyes on the stars so that you don't end up with your nose in the gutter.

LL: *Crime, Justice and Protecting the Public* embodies a very fundamental statement about the future. Are you sympathetic?

PT: The White Paper reflects beautifully the problem of punishment in the community. It is a political attempt to reassure the community that punishment is going on – apparently a political necessity, because we are obsessed with the notion that there is a relationship between the severity of the punishment and the incidence of crime. There is not a scrap of evidence to support that. We suffer from a national neurosis that we must punish people so as to keep us all in order.

LL: Do you agree that if people break the law we must punish them?

PT: Punishment is vital. I have no argument about that. It is an essential part of the rehabilitative process. You have to control people – civil service orders are a good example. But that control is like a punishment. If one goes to the theology of it, the wages of sin is death. The more I hurt you, the more I kill myself. That principle, I believe, holds good for all human beings. What punishment can do, and in the end can only do, is to signal to me that my behaviour towards other people is in turn destroying me. In an ideal world, before dealing with an offender, one would always ask: Are my actions likely to produce that effect? The whole penological system is an appalling reflection of that theology. Prisoners are our children. You have to come back to basics and ask the basic questions.

LL: Would you say that there is a specifically religious approach? Should any good Humanist say the same?

PT: To be truly human is, in the end, to be truly divine. If we see within another human being something of the potential and the image of God, it becomes alarmingly difficult to destroy them.

LL: Such an enlightened former minister as Lord Windlesham and the new White Paper both agree that rehabilitation has been discredited. On the other hand, some people say that it has not been discredited [see pages 155/6]; it has just never been tried.

PT: It is all a nonsense, because it depends which criteria you use. You don't say that medical treatment has failed because people die. If a violent person is treated with dignity, thought and care, and if he returns to society and commits a crime, but not a violent crime again, this shows incredible progress. It does not show that prison has failed.

LL: Coming back to your actual life as a governor. Did you find any conflict between those high principles and the system you were called upon to administer?

PT: No, I did not find any conflict. Prisoners in the

end know within themselves that certain be- haviour ends in certain results. Prison is like a game in a way – so long as you play the game by the rules, nobody objects very much. The game is that you are the boss and they are not the boss. There is an understanding as to how the game is played. Prison life succeeds by games – minor manipulations of the system happening all the time.

When I was at Maidstone and going through a bad patch, the Director of Prisons said to me: 'I have always believed, Peter, that Maidstone is one of our most difficult prisons to govern. It is easy to bang people up and apply the rules rigidly. That's easy. But when it comes to trying to be creative and allow prisoners some freedom of choice behind the glass wall – that inevitably gives rise to problems and stress.'

LL: One problem: some prisoners can be kept shut up in their cells for twenty-three hours a day. Is this a problem of resources or of attitude? How could one provide enough resources to enable people to spend evenings out of their cells?

PT: It is about both to some degree, but I am optimis- tic. I believe that we are beginning on a whole new adventure in the prison system. Fresh Start has made prison officers salaried as opposed to wage earners – that is a beginning. The weak- ness, and it is a very serious weakness, is that Fresh Start has not been sufficiently balanced by a change of emphasis in the nature of the task the officer is asked to do. We need to upgrade every- thing an officer is asked to do, so that a man can feel proud to be a prison officer – because he is doing something worthwhile and creative.

Peter Timms ended by illustrating yet again his undying faith in the ordinary prison officer, never forgetting that he began his career as such a one.

PT: Eighty per cent of prison officers want to do something creative for prisoners. They don't just want to lock prisoners up. If we do not accommodate this need, we shall miss the opportunity that Fresh Start presents for us, and we have not got a lot of time. We need to train our people and we need to signal to them what is important. In some ways a total rethink of the role of the prison officer in prison is what is called for.

David Evans

David Evans is the General Secretary of the Prison Officers' Association. He is a former prison officer and, before that, came close to being a junior Welsh International at rugby football (a scrum half). In 1970 he became Assistant Secretary to the Prison Officers' Association and its General Secretary in 1979. No one involved in penal reform can be unaware that he has introduced to the full extent of his power a new atmosphere in the POA. He is an idealist and, it may be added, an optimist. He considers that ultimately the interests of prisoners and prison officers are identical. That may be far from the reality as perceived by prison officers and prisoners, but in the deepest sense it must be right.

In recent years the statements of the Prison Officers' Association have come much closer to the views of penal reformers. About a year before I interviewed David Evans, they published an important document headed *Inmate Regimes – A Service in Decline*. I quote only the initial paragraph:

> Over the recent months the National Executive Committee of the POA has been involved in considerable debate with the Home Office Prison Department regarding the state of the Prison Service. We have been raising on a continual basis the effects of overcrowding on a system which is creaking and the impossibility of fulfilling regime commitments to the prisoner population due to the undermanning in 'Fresh Start' terms. To understand the extent of the problem it is essential to accept the self-evident truth that part and parcel of this mosaic is the serious effects overcrowding has on the prison service.

David Evans was brutally frank about the present situation. 'There is a prison crisis at present. In some prisons people are deprived of the basic human decencies [a change of clothing and a bath once a week], due to the overcrowding. The prison population is dropping – but will that continue?' He pointed out that there were two categories of prisoner, adults and young offenders under eighteen. Within less than a year there was the prospect of the Prison Department being able to close between five and eleven young offenders' prisons. The Prison Department would use that as an opportunity to economize, but the POA would see it as an opportunity to provide places for people from overcrowded prisons. The staff in adult and young offenders' prisons were interchangeable. A good libertarian Home Secretary could impose his will on the Prison Department – that is, on the senior civil servants who advise the minister.

'The worst prisons,' David Evans maintained, 'should be closed altogether. One should build good and close bad prisons as a general principle. There is understaffing, partly due to over-crowding. An increase in prison staff is being requested to provide better conditions for the prisoners. Twenty years ago in Penton-ville, there were hardly any prisoners locked in their cells – today everybody is locked up after 5.30 p.m.'

Security is a major problem. David Evans was particularly interesting on the subject, including the security of prison officers. There has been no major review of security since that of Mount-batten in the 1960s. Prison officers would feel more secure if prisoners were given their statutory rights – education, leisure and so on. The interests of the prisoners and of the officers are the same, after all. The Prison Department have turned their backs on the fact that prisoners can be rehabilitated.

'They *can* be rehabilitated,' he asserted, 'but if they are locked up for most of the day with no work, there is no chance of rehabilitation. In Pentonville twenty years ago, there was a liaison service to ensure that on release there were jobs and places to stay for everyone. The Prison Department should have made this work throughout the system, but no time, resources or imagination have been employed. Work and a place to live are the essential things. Aftercare should start in prison. The prison and probation services should be one. The two services must collaborate.'

Naturally I raised the question with him as to how far prison officers should be allowed to play a constructive role, and whether they are capable of doing so. The vast majority, he assured me, could indeed play such a role. There should be shared experience about the needs of prisoners. 'This won't happen yet, but even as things are much could be done.' Sanitation, he pointed out, was a basic human decency and a lot of money was being spent on it. In five years we should see a rapid improvement. He agreed with Judge Tumim that decent physical conditions did much to improve moral attitudes.

I asked him about alternatives to prison. He agreed that there should be more punishment in the community, although he was totally opposed to electronic tagging.

'Many people in the community who are mentally deranged should be in Broadmoor or in another secure hospital. At present they inevitably end up in prison. The clinically insane and the socially inadequate should be removed from prison. The latter, as in Germany, should be sent to live on farms where they can provide a service to the community.

'The remand prison population could be drastically reduced by applying the 110-day rule as in Scotland. Prisoners would have to be brought to trial within 110 days, instead of as now often being left on remand in prison for more than a year. More bail hostels and bail information schemes would make a big difference. Measures such as these could bring about within a short space of time a substantial reduction in the prison population. Only after that happens can you treat people properly, give them work and introduce them to an employer.'

Like an increasing number of prison reformers, David Evans has turned against parole, I am sorry to say. 'Parole should be abolished as it is unfair and only suitable for middle-class prisoners. Half remission should replace it.'

David Evans's final thoughts resembled those of most of my witnesses: 'The judges and their sentencing policies are the major problem.'

At the time of writing (June 1990), relations between the Prison Officers' Association and the government are very poor. I hold in my hand *Gate Lodge, The Prison Officers' Magazine* (June 1990). The first leading article is headed: 'Annual Conference 1990. National Chairman, John Bartell, calls upon Senior Prison Department

Officials to resign.' The General Secretary began his address in this way:

Mr Chairman and Colleagues,

The last seven weeks have been the most traumatic, the most trying and the most tragic ever experienced by the Prison Service.

The period has seen Manchester's Strangeways prison almost totally destroyed in consequence of riot and siege. . . . In total, thirty jails have experienced significant disturbances, but nearly all prison staff have in some way been affected as a result.

The Prison Officers' Association believe with every fibre of their being that prisons today are grossly understaffed. It has been pointed out that the ratio of officers to prisoners is more than twice as high in 1990 as it was in 1950. The POA are convinced that mismanagement by the Prison Department has nullified this much improved ratio. For myself, I await a thorough investigation of this issue by Lord Justice Woolf and his expert advisers. My sympathies are with the prison officers. I hope that their views prove to be justified.

Alan Eastwood

Alan Eastwood is the Chairman of the Police Federation. A Sergeant, he joined the Metropolitan Police in 1965 and has been National Chairman of the Police Federation since 1985. He served as a uniformed officer in East London and is married with five children. He is also just the kind of man one hopes to find in such a position: well built, firm but friendly, fully prepared for our interview and a fine host at the lunch which followed. We met at his headquarters in Surbiton.

Alan Eastwood pointed out that officially the police are not concerned with the punishment of criminals after conviction. Their official duty is to detect and apprehend. He admitted, however, that the police are only human to feel anger when a convicted person receives a much lighter sentence than his offence seems to warrant.

Subject to certain qualifications, his answers to my main questions were in line with the general evidence received from other witnesses. Yes, there are too many men and women in prison. Yes, many minor offenders ought not to be there. Yes, violent men should be sent to prison. Yes, he agreed with the idea of prison as a place of character-training. Every prison officer would be delighted if prisoners emerged from prison as law-abiding citizens.

In regard to sentencing, however, he showed more confidence in the judiciary than others who gave evidence. He placed particular emphasis on the need to preserve the *discretion* of the judges. It was only by the use of that discretion that a judge could take into account the individual characteristics of the prisoner before him. Magistrates, on the other hand, were much too ready to follow the rule book in a mechanical fashion.

I pressed him in regard to his suggestion that those convicted of violent crime should be kept in prison until it was safe to let them out. He countered with the retort, which he repeated more than once, that the police had much confidence in the Parole Board.

They could be relied on to release a prisoner when the time was ripe.

He said with obvious sincerity that he was proud of the police as they are today. The considerable intake of graduates was one feature, but by no means the only feature, of a new and more intelligent image. 'The old bobby on the beat is sometimes seen through rose-tinted spectacles, but of course the reality was always somewhat different. Nevertheless, that old bobby embodied certain values we mustn't lose sight of.'

When I asked him about the *prevention* of crime, he said that everything depended on the cooperation of the general public. This must be a two-way affair, involving mutual confidence between police and public. He pointed to impressive joint efforts to educate schoolchildren about the meaning of crime and the role of the police. In reply to a question, he said that it was usually helpful to wear uniform in speaking to small, but not older, children.

The most disquieting feature of the scene today, he felt, was the growth of violent crime and the increased use of firearms by criminals. There was no doubt that the danger to a policeman's life had seriously increased. The police themselves felt that, as a consequence, they were being pushed in the direction of being armed. He pointed out that the British police were the only police force in Europe not armed. (My query: 'What about the Irish Republic?') All the wisest heads in the force were against our police being armed. It would certainly destroy any confidence-building with the public.

In this connection there arose (not to my surprise) one point of serious difference between myself and the Chairman. He emphasized that the Police Federation had been opposed to the abolition of capital punishment and by a clear majority were in favour of its restoration. Its use in practice would depend on the discretion of the judge. He did not seem confident that it would, in fact, be restored. A senior police officer told me at lunch that the younger recruits were much less favourable to capital punishment than their elders.

The Chairman said his Federation were convinced that the abolition of capital punishment had increased the volume of violent crime, and in particular had encouraged the carrying of firearms by criminals. He was, of course, aware of counter-arguments, but he was speaking on behalf of those 'at the sharp end'. He added that the Prison Officers' Association agreed with the Police Federation in this matter. So did the Police Superintendents' Association. On the other hand, the Association of Chief Constables were divided and Sir Peter Imbert, the Commissioner of the Metropolitan Police, was opposed to restoration. Alan Eastwood may have thought, though he did not say so, that Chief Constables were further from the sharp end.

We agreed in applauding the objective of the government's plans for punishment in the community. We were both aware of the vital part that would have to be played by the probation service. I was sorry and surprised to learn that relations between the police and the probation service were far from satisfactory at the present time. I can only hope that they will have improved by the time that this book sees the light of day.

We touched briefly on the Strangeways riots. At the time of the interview, there were still seven men on the roof after a fortnight. The police, it appears, could have forced a surrender. The Chairman did not offer an opinion on whether that course of action could have been taken. He was not surprised that there should have been an outbreak in Strangeways, given the over-crowding and the many hours spent in the cells. I think that the degree of violence surprised him, like everyone else.

II
Penal Reformers

Peter Thompson

Peter Thompson is the founder of the Matthew Trust for Mental Patients and Victims of Crime. I have described him elsewhere as 'unique' and I will not withdraw that accolade. He has been a friend of mine since 1958. Our first public work together was through the Pakenham/Thompson Committee, which Peter founded in 1959. This committee produced a report which had much influence on the setting-up of NACRO (National Association for the Care and Resettlement of Offenders) and the acceptance by the probation service of a national responsibility for ex-prisoners.

When Peter became a governor of a State school, he entered *The Guinness Book of Records* as the first ex-patient of Broadmoor to achieve such a position. As founder and continuous inspiration of the Matthew Trust, he has provided unswerving encouragement to all who break down in health and pay the penalty.

I began by asking Peter whether he was reasonably satisfied with the way abnormal offenders were treated now. He replied by saying that the spirit of the 1959 Mental Health Act had been lost sight of in subsequent Mental Health Acts. For example, the Home Office now used the facilities of the National Health Service to extend prison sentences by transferring prisoners, once they had completed their sentence in prison, to special hospitals. In Broadmoor, to make another point, the emphasis was on chemotherapy, whereas the emphasis should be on psychotherapy. The latter, however, is regarded as being too expensive. The Secretary of State for Health may claim that patients are being discharged whole and well, but because 99 per cent of them have not received the treatment which they were sent to hospital to receive, they are coming out stabilized but not cured. 'I did not get over my problem when I came out of Broadmoor,' Peter said.

Peter laid much emphasis on the next point. 'The majority of people who go to special hospitals should not be convicted, but should be just assessed. When you go to a special hospital you are not sentenced; you are detained until you are better, under one of the Detention Orders of the Mental Health Acts.

'If you are fit to plead you are convicted depending on your clinical state. But if somebody merits detention under a Mental Health Act in a special hospital, there is a moral case that they should not be convicted. It is impossible to entertain the idea of conviction in the case of somebody who has a substantial degree of mental disorder. There cannot be a question of conviction if one considers the true spirit of the Mental Health Act. If you are unwell and are regarded as being seriously unwell, although you may not be unfit to plead because of insanity, it is difficult to reconcile conviction with a disturbed mind. I myself should never have been convicted. I am not saying that I should not have been detained in Broadmoor – that was a humanitarian act. Sentencing me to an open psychiatric hospital would have made me worse. But sending me to Broadmoor was a humane gesture.'

Peter referred me to a lecture, *The Abnormal Offender in Society*, which he gave to the Cleveland Criminology Society. There he stated unequivocally:

My view is opposite to Lord Longford's. We should no longer consider punishment as an essential means of dealing with offenders. Instead we should consider admonishment, as this view breaks away from the Victorian era and would allow for the recognition of influences imposed on offenders, not heard of in Victorian times, prior to the offence. An offender should no longer be seen as a criminal reject of society, but as a casualty within society, a society that has amorally pursued a dated course of retribution. The concept of admonishment allows for the offender to be given due regard in terms of his natural dignity. The offender is thereby not debased as a human being and is more receptive to a reformative approach.

LL: I understand that you think the key word is 'admonishment'. Spelling this out a little more, would you describe this as a 'caring rebuke', as to a child?

PT: The connotation is that you still respect a person's basic integrity, and that integrity needs to be kept intact so that there is a basis on which to build a reformative and rehabilitative programme.

LL: But where a serious crime has been committed, does this mean that you would sentence the person to imprisonment?

PT: Most crimes are not violent crimes. Those are in the minority.

LL: Most of the people now in prison would have to be given a 'caring rebuke'?

PT: All of them would be given this caring rebuke which is the foundation for a totally different philosophy towards conviction, detention and rehabilitation. The Victorian principle of vindictiveness has failed and has proved to be a cancer in the penal system. My view of a caring rebuke would be the origin of an era of new thinking, rather than treating an offender as a third-class citizen. No matter what the crime, you still regard them *as equal to oneself.*

Offenders should be treated as sick people. The offender, in the philosophy which should replace the old one, should receive the same natural respect as the judge and the prosecuting counsel – which does not mean that he should not be detained in prison. But prison society – the management, staff and specialists – should have a totally different emotional, spiritual and intellectual regard for a wounded spirit rather than a criminal one.

LL: You mean that you would approach them in the same way as the special hospitals do?

PT: I see no difference.

LL: This is obviously a very important point. You do not blame people when they are mentally disturbed. Are we going to say that this is to be the attitude towards all criminals?

PT: More often than not the offender, too, becomes a victim through the process of committing the offence. The offence is a symptom of the problem and is equal to the victim the offender may have hurt.

LL: So you don't draw a distinction between the treatment of the mentally disturbed offender and others?

PT: If one is asking society, the penal system and the judiciary to adopt this philosophy, quite naturally society will say: what is in it for us, if we are to change our views? Cynicism creeps in.

LL: What effect is this going to have on society generally?

PT: To get the best safeguards for the public in terms of the patients in secure hospitals, you have to apply psychiatric methods instead of chemotherapy. In order to ensure the well-being of society when someone is discharged from prison, you must have somebody who is intact, not somebody who for ten years or more has been the subject of retribution.

        The recidivist rate among the patients in special hospitals is much lower than those who come out of prison. The recidivist rate for first offenders is something like 80 per cent or more, but that for offenders who enter special hospitals is more like 3 or 5 per cent. In special hospitals there is a caring, not a retributive, attitude, whereas the person in prison is constantly being reminded that he is less than a third-class citizen in society.

LL: Just one more question. If people ask: Why have prisons? – most would say that if you don't have them more crime would be committed. Prisons help to keep crime within limits. But the argument for prisons is that people must be treated as responsible for their actions and punished if they break the rules.

PT: You would still need prisons, but you would need a totally different philosophy of management. The majority of offenders are not violent, not murderers or rapists. You are talking about extreme situations.

LL: Are you going to say they are not responsible?

PT: Most people, if not all, who commit an antisocial act damage a third party. The person who commits that act is as much a victim as the victim who has been offended by that person.

LL: I find that difficult to swallow.

PT: It is recognized that somebody who has lived in foster homes and has been deprived of parental love inevitably makes a bad father and should hesitate about getting married and having children. Life is too short to indulge in the luxury of blaming anybody. The most important thing is to reform, to change the values or redirect the values of the person who has offended, so that they can play a positive and constructive role in society.

LL: Would you agree that your programme would demand vastly greater resources?

PT: The crime rate is appallingly high in this country – serious crimes are leaping up, especially those by a previous offender. So you must have both human and material resources for this change in penal philosophy.

LL: The abnormal offender in recent years: more people are being sent to prison nowadays than some years ago when they would have been sent to hospital.

PT: Recent legislation has made it possible for hospitals to refuse.

Professor Terence Morris

Professor Terence Morris ('Terry' to me for many years of friendship) is of special interest among eminent criminologists. As Professor of Social Institutions at the University of London he has won a distinguished position in his profession, but he has never ceased to search for reconciliation between criminology and Christian, in his case Catholic, theology.

When I interviewed him, I approached him not only as a representative criminologist, but also as a Catholic and as someone who has always thought for himself in an individual fashion.

'My first impressions of prison were formed very distinctly when I was about six years of age,' Terence Morris told me. 'A former prisoner came to visit my father and explained to me about hard labour. I took out the geographic map of London and picked out all the London prisons. Eventually, between the ages of eight and twelve, I must have cycled round to look at all of them.'

He went on: 'Intellectually, what I feel about the prison system is that it represents that part of the exercise of authority which is so frequently manifested in injustice. The idea of injustice strikes me very forcibly. My experience of school was that people were always being punished in excess.'

I put it to Terry that what he was saying was that punishment and injustice had a fundamental connection.

'I have been aware of it all my life, and increasingly aware of it as a schoolboy,' he replied. 'I suppose I was a bit clever. It struck me that the kind of people who resorted to beating were on the whole people who were not intelligent. The best masters were those who stimulated people.'

Terry went on to explain that he grew up in a very articulate, politically orientated family. His grandmother was a staunch supporter of the Co-operative movement. He was taken to political meetings from a quite early age. In 1948, he wandered into a meeting organized by the Howard League for Penal Reform. He got hold of a book, a seminal one in its time, by Fenner (later, Lord) Brockway and Stephen Hobhouse: *English Prisons Today*.

He felt then that he had to become involved with prisons. He joined the Howard League. He has been a member of it for about forty years and is now Vice-President.

He singled out two main issues: penal reform and capital punishment. 'Once you are locked in on these two issues, you are locked in for life.' He became a student of criminology and fell under the influence of Margery Fry, who had just given up as secretary to the Howard League. He became a prison visitor (1952/3) in Wormwood Scrubs. His prisoners were long-term ones, half of them 'lifers' reprieved from the gallows.

'In about my second week, having been warned not to talk to prisoners about their sentences, I was given a chap to visit and went into his cell. I took in some cigarettes as a symbolic subversion of the system. The man said straight away: "I have not been able to talk to anybody, nobody at all." He had just spent three weeks in the condemned cell, followed by a short spell in the prison hospital. There had been no one during all that time for him to talk to. He was about twenty-one – and there was I, a privileged undergraduate. He actually spoke to me about his feelings while in the death cell and what it had been like throughout those three dreadful weeks. It was truly shocking, leaving me with a sense, in a curious sort of way, that what I had to do was to speak for people like that. I got stuck with it. I felt it was my vocation – I would never make a social worker.'

Terry realized early on that the penal system was, in his words, 'part of the total political process'. But for many years, there was a political consensus in the House of Commons. This has in recent times been broken up by Margaret Thatcher and 'Thatcherism'. About both he spoke very severely. 'Things which were previously regarded as dishonourable have now become respectable. One Tory MP announced in the House of Commons, "the homeless have turned their backs on society". It would be far truer to say that society has turned its back on the homeless.' He was much concerned about the undermining of the higher civil service. 'Until recently, there were a number of wise, thoughtful, calm, reflective civil servants in the Home Office, but their position has been much weakened.'

I called Terry's attention to one possible benefit of the government's passion for economy: 'Don't you think there could be a beneficial outcome from this desire not to spend money on prisons?'

He replied sharply enough. 'Can a result be regarded as good even when it derives from an evil intention? The real question is: Should any part of human suffering constitute the source of financial profit for anyone else? Thatcherites talk of a restoration of Victorian values, thereby revealing their ignorance. Our Victorian forebears were people who were hard-headed, totally dedicated to a business ethic and the value of money, but they were certainly concerned with moral rectitude.

'Basically, Thatcherites regard public expenditure as something intrinsically undesirable. You reduce it to a minimum, and where you cannot do so, you distance yourself through the notion of government by agency. You privatize.'

I turned more directly to crime. I pointed out that thirty years ago there were only three criminologists in this country. Had the immense expansion of criminology since then affected policy either in the prevention of crime or the treatment of criminals? Terry replied by paying a high tribute to the work of the Home Office Research and Planning Unit. The work there represented the best in the whole of Europe. He made three points in illustration of this thesis:

1. Ministers of whatever political persuasion have had to take on board the advice which stems from civil service advisers, as a result of research initiated by the Home Office: for example, in regard to policing, race relations and time spent on remand.
2. The unit sets a standard or benchmark against which all other criminological work is now measured.
3. It is now impossible for the two really powerful interest groups in criminal justice, the police and the judiciary, to be entirely a law unto themselves.

I put it to him that the most constructive idea that the government were now propounding was 'punishment in the community'. Had the Research and Planning Unit had anything to do with this? Terry Morris was guarded: 'Difficult to say how much. It is perfectly obvious that there might have been some significant input.' In his eyes, the statements of the present Home Secretary, Mr David Waddington, are much more carefully researched, much more moderate and much more hemmed-in by statistical caveats. Morris permits himself to envisage Thatcherism as one of those fireworks which burn brightly, glow and then slowly decline. (As I correct the proofs of this book in December 1990, that decline is now much closer to reality.)

'What would you do if you were in power and had a free hand?' I asked him. 'In what direction would you move in terms of the reconstruction of penal policy?'

'I would split my activities,' he replied. 'I would look to see what could usefully be done organizationally on the one hand, and in terms of policy on the other. Organizationally, I would like to set up a Correctional Agency. I would like to see it have responsibility for all those who had been before the courts, including the mentally disordered, so that there would no longer be the scandal of prisons having to look after disturbed offenders whom the doctors in mental hospitals decline to accept as patients. Its activities would need to be clearly divided between custodial and non-custodial options.

'While I would leave the judiciary alone as far as possible,' he continued, 'I would like to get away from single-sentencers, whether stipendiary magistrates or high court judges. I should like sentencing to be done by panels of three – either three magistrates or a judge and two magistrates – seen to have equal status. It would prevent individual judges, like Judge Pickles, from getting into a "pickle".'

In terms of policy he would 'leave the judiciary alone, but proceed to introduce a Criminal Justice Bill of first importance'. It would introduce a presumption in sentencing. The case for a custodial sentence would have to be argued convincingly before it could be awarded. Instead, the offender should be given an opportunity of making reparation for his offence. The reparative aspect 'should take precedence over any kind of punitive intervention'. Instead of going to prison, a person convicted of dangerous driving, for example, should serve every weekend for the next two years as a porter in the casualty department of the local hospital. Every victim is, in a sense, 'the victim of every offender'. If somebody is seeking reparation, it is a kind of collective reparation.

Terry Morris believes that we should establish a hierarchy of priorities in the list of criminal offences. 'The motto that everybody, every Home Secretary and every legislator, ought to have on their desk is this: "You cannot legislate to make men moral. All you can do is to try to control the worst excesses of their behaviour." '

I asked him whether, in addition to what he had said, he had any distinctively Christian message. He surprised me by answering: 'I believe – what I would hold as definitively Christian – that there is something quite evil in the world, a personal devil. I do actually believe that some people have been taken over by the devil. I have known mentally ill people who have been possessed. I don't think it happens all that often, but manifests itself in what the Italian criminologists call "the absence of probity". When you get a particularly horrible crime, that is the work of the devil.'

Terry rounded off his Christian thoughts in this way: 'There is no one who did not have a redemption ticket bought for him on Calvary. I see redemption as being like an outing – you have to claim the ticket already bought for you in your name. It is there waiting for you, but you have got to go and claim it. There is one waiting for all of us. We are all redeemed. Those who do not experience redemption in the afterlife are those who do not bother to collect their ticket in this one.'

When I myself was being instructed for the Catholic Church, I asked the great Jesuit, Father Martin d'Arcy, whether one had to believe in Hell. 'Yes,' he replied, 'but you need not believe that, in the mercy of God, anyone ever goes there.' I hope and believe that Terry Morris, most merciful of men, shares that view.

I end by recording part of his reconciliation of criminology and theology. 'Punishment is what is deserved from wrongdoing, but it need not be negative. Contrition – the genuine expression of sorrow – is to be distinguished from remorse which is generally a feeling of "I am sorry I did this and I wish that I had never done it, on account of all the trouble it has brought me". There can be no absolution without contrition, which must include a firm purpose cf amendment *not to do it again*, whether or not that should be the case. *Punishment* or *penance* is the symbolic act on the part of the offender which completes the process.'

In the case of sin, absolution does not necessarily have to be followed by penance, since Christ suffered for the sins of the whole world on the Cross, but if I understand Professor Morris correctly, that does not absolve the criminal who breaks the law from liability to punishment, where the total interests of the State require it.

Paul Cavadino

Paul Cavadino, a Senior Information Officer of NACRO (National Association for the Care and Resettlement of Offenders), is like myself a member of the All-Party Penal Affairs Group of the Houses of Parliament. I am well aware of the enormous debt that group owes to him, their Secretary. He is known to some of us as the 'Penal Encyclopaedia'. Paul is aged forty-one and a Catholic. He was educated at St Michael's Jesuit College, Leeds, read Law at Balliol and has worked for NACRO since 1972.

Though receiving considerable financial support from government departments, NACRO has remained remarkably independent. 'Our main function is the resettlement of offenders,' he told me. 'We have two hundred projects providing accommodation, employment and training, education and other practical services for offenders. That is our main purpose. In addition we provide information, having a thriving information and research office.'

NACRO's policies on penal reform are set out in a comprehensive document, *Prisons and Penal Policy*. They are broadly in line with the *Joint Manifesto for Penal Reform* (see pages 113/14). There are, however, additional features, such as the establishment of a National Criminal Policy Committee. I asked Paul Cavadino whether NACRO had played a large part in the production and promotion of the *Joint Manifesto*. 'Certainly,' he replied.

Lord Longford:	Is a National Criminal Policy Committee intended to produce a comprehensive criminal policy as an alternative to what others have suggested, namely a Sentencing Council?
Paul Cavadino:	This committee would bring together a policy on crime and offenders generally. The Sentencing Council would give guidance to the courts on sentencing, it would be part of the Court of Appeal – quite a different thing. The Sentencing Council would be headed by the Lord Chief Justice and

would comprise judges, but the judges would also have alongside them magistrates, prison governors and academic penologists, so that the input into sentencing guidance would draw on much broader experience.

LL: The National Criminal Policy Committee – would it include ministers?

PC: I would see it as including ministers, but in practice most of the work would be done by officials and senior members of the agencies concerned.

LL: If there were no prisons at all, there would be more crime. Would you not say that prison is a deterrent?

PC: I think its general deterrent effect on the overall crime rate is minimal, for two reasons. First, research into prison sentencing in different countries suggests that tougher or more lenient sentences have no discernible effect on the overall rate of crime. And secondly, many serious crimes are committed in emotional circumstances and it is highly unlikely that thoughts of the consequences of their action enter into the minds of the offenders at the time.

LL: Do you really mean that if you got rid of prison altogether there would be no crime?

PC: The effect of prison on the rate of crime is very small. Many people would not commit crime regardless of penalties. There are some offenders who might be deterred by the fact of imprisonment, but if we think of people who do commit offences, many do not calculate or plan them in a rational manner – many crimes are impulsive and not carefully planned. Those who do plan their crimes also plan to avoid being caught and expect to get away with it.

LL: In your view, then, the effect of prison as a deterrent is minimal. What is the argument for sending anyone to prison? The government's view is that violent people should be sent to prison. Is prison more of a deterrent to violent people than to others?

PC: The only justification is to protect the public by taking violent offenders out of circulation. If you simply wanted to punish people, prison has so many ill effects that you would look for another method of punishment. If we are talking about prison, then the only rational argument is to keep violent people out of circulation. Violence and sexual offences are worse than theft.

LL: Hooligans are violent, but I don't think they are worse than a City fraudster, for example.

PC: It is not always necessary to imprison for minor offences of violence; it is much better to deal with them in other ways.

LL: Do you wish to say anything about the theory of imprisonment? It has become a rather relevant question now. The government are saying that retribution is the dominant factor: the seriousness of the offence and the culpability of the offender should be clearly related to the severity of punishment. What do you feel about people being given their just deserts?

PC: It is not right to leave proportionality out of account. The gravity of the offence and the severity of punishment should be related, otherwise the punishment system would be devoid of much of its credibility. There should be a strict correlation between the gravity of the offence and the degree of punishment. If retribution were left out, then sentencing would be just social engineering devoid of moral content.

LL: Punishment in proportion to the seriousness of the crime should be the principal focus. How do you react?

PC: It is impossible to defend imprisonment on retributive grounds for many minor offences. At the moment people are being punished more severely than the offence warrants. If you have a retributive policy, it provides a very good argument for reducing the use of prison a great deal.

LL: Even assuming that retribution should be the dominant factor, surely far too many people are sent to prison? There are a great many people in prison who don't deserve it.

PC: One of my criticisms is that the government appear to depart from the principle of retribution when they propose in the White Paper *Crime, Justice and Protecting the Public* that violent or sexual offenders should be imprisoned for longer than the offence deserves. I consider that in this way they are deviating from their own principles.

LL: But is the actual assertion of retribution the right approach?

PC: I have a great deal of sympathy; many people are punished far too harshly.

LL: You mean that, properly handled, retribution would be a humanitarian idea?

PC: It would have a very important limiting effect on what the courts are allowed to do.

LL: But this is going much further. Is this new emphasis in your opinion healthy?

PC: Well, the White Paper's emphasis goes too far in making retribution the principal focus. But it *could* do more good than harm – too many people are punished too severely. If it could be worked out intellectually – people often use retribution incorrectly as meaning vengeance for its own sake. Used properly, in proportion to the seriousness of the crime, retribution would scale down the level of punishment.

LL: Barbara Wootton did not like psychiatrists. She used to say that you cannot judge the degree of culpability.

PC: You must start with the seriousness of the offence and this is really very important. If someone commits an offence under great provocation, you cannot deal with him in the same way as with somebody who deliberately planned and ruthlessly carried out a similar type of offence – you must allow for mitigating circumstances. If we are trying to administer a system of justice, we must do our best to deal with people fairly.

LL: Would you agree that the general collapse of the rehabilitative ideal has left people with retribution as the only alternative? Do you feel that it is right to reject the rehabilitative ideal and that prison is no longer part of the picture?

PC: The pendulum is swinging back a little from the writing off of rehabilitation. All of us who work with offenders believe that people can change and can be helped to change, otherwise there would be little point in the work we are doing. In NACRO we have never taken the defeatist view.

LL: You think that people can be helped to change much better outside than inside? But then the question arises: how far have you got the same control as in prison? Can supervision in the community be effective?

PC: Yes, as we know from research and experience. The Home Office research into parole supervision shows that it reduces the likelihood of offenders committing further crimes. Interestingly enough, whether it is the supervision or the threat of recall, it does reduce the likelihood of re-offending quite remarkably. There has been quite a lot of local research into probation day centres and intermediate treatment schemes for young offenders, which has shown that they are more successful in reducing re-offending than custody – more successful than either custody or complete freedom.

LL: So when we say that the pendulum is swinging back, it is really swinging back to punishment outside prison?

PC: The good thing about swinging away from the traditional idea of rehabilitation is that no one has any excuse for sending people to prison in the misguided belief that it will improve them. But the danger is that if the rehabilitative idea goes completely, then prison officers become demoralized and see no point in their efforts. Prison officers were very put out when probation officers came into prisons. In NACRO we are training prison officers in twelve prisons to help prisoners and advise them on problems such as housing and employment on release.

LL: About parole: the government are broadly following the recommendations of the recent Carlisle conclusions. I am on the whole against Carlisle. On the one hand the report is based on the expectation that sentences will be slightly reduced, but if no new ideas evolve, it will increase sentences. What is NACRO's view?

PC: NACRO would like to see a modified version of the Carlisle proposals with automatic release for prisoners serving up to four years after one-third, instead of one-half, of the sentence had been served. It would have been possible to do a lot of good things that Carlisle suggested while reducing instead of increasing the prison population. The White Paper acknowledges that there will be more recalls for those released on parole, so Carlisle will increase the prison population.

LL: I don't regard that as at all progressive.

Stephen Shaw

The Prison Reform Trust, set up in 1981, has made a remarkable impact in the last nine years. It is undoubtedly one of the most effective pressure groups in the country. They claim with justice that there is an ever increasing recognition of the importance of penal reform. If this is so, few would deny the Prison Reform Trust a considerable part of the credit.

The Trust's Director, Stephen Shaw, is thirty-seven years old. He trained as an economist and his doctorate was on unemployment and wage bargaining. After teaching in technical colleges, he became a research officer in NACRO (National Association for the Care and Resettlement of Offenders), studying the economics of the penal system. Later, he worked for a year in the Home Office. The Prison Reform Trust and Stephen Shaw seem to have been designed for one another.

Shaw's general approach to penal reform is expressed in his Fabian pamphlet *Conviction Politics, A Plan for Penal Policy* (October 1987), in which he points to what seem to him the fundamental flaws in well-known theories of punishment – those, for example, of rehabilitation, deterrence and containment. He notices without enthusiasm a movement back to punishment as a response to the perception that nothing works. Nevertheless, he remains an optimist about the possibilities of a planned penal system. I quote one paragraph from his conclusions:

> A planned penal system should set targets to minimise the use of custody, reduce the number of sentencing options and impose tighter statutory guidelines in the courts. Preventing the excesses of the judiciary is fundamental, and aside from statutory restrictions, which would in fact mean building upon existing restrictions, there is much to be said for some form of Sentencing Council, to establish a national framework for sentencing reform and provide consistent guidance for the courts. Within such a Sentencing Council, the judiciary would properly enjoy considerable representation. But membership would reflect expertise from throughout the criminal justice process.

Stephen Shaw was more optimistic than I expected. He finds much of his inspiration from a modern application of liberty, equality and fraternity. They point the way to a society in which human rights are preserved for all, including prisoners.

'The political auguries at the moment are better than they have been, and Labour may be in power in two years,' he told me. 'There is every chance that criminal justice could be the first major piece of legislation in home affairs.

'The Labour alternative White Paper is a good, reforming document taking in the need for a Sentencing Council, minimum standards in prison conditions, the need for an independent disciplinary system and an ombudsman to deal with complaints. The White Paper would change the life-sentence system. It is a distillation of what the various lobbying organizations have been saying for the last ten to fifteen years.'

But Stephen Shaw was also optimistic about the present Conservative government. 'When David Waddington was appointed Home Secretary, his being pro capital punishment was regarded as the litmus test. Instead, he has embraced the policies of his predecessor, Douglas Hurd.' His praise for the government White Paper, *Crime, Justice and Protecting the Public*, was qualified: 'The government could take reasonable pride in the fall in the prison population and in setting up a strategy for bringing it under control. However, the emphasis on punishment and re-tribution as the sole goal and principal focus is distasteful, so is the stress on "just deserts".'

Criminal justice should have many objectives and there should be concern for the needs of the offender as well as those of the victim. Stephen Shaw insists that there should be a statutory framework for sentencing which should be built up over the years. According to present plans, legislation will be brought forward at the end of 1990. There will be guidelines which the Court of Appeal will have to interpret. Much will depend on which cases are appealed and of course on the wisdom of the judges and the Court of Appeal.

Stephen Shaw, as I expected, insisted on the need for a Sentencing Council. He agreed, however, that there were a number of possible models. He seemed to prefer the original one which would be an adjunct to the Court of Appeal, but feared that the judiciary would not agree. Alternatively, there could be a separate advisory body which would be politically more feasible, as the judiciary might be expected to approve.

'We are out of line,' he said, 'with European prison practice. We should bring our sentencing policy into line with the Dutch or Germans.' He informed me of what I had not realized, that prison riots were the turning-point in bringing about the German reforms. He summed up: 'Our prison population should be reduced by many thousands. Judges should be consistent in their sentencing policy. What has been done with young offenders could be done with adults. There has been no political backlash from the legislation making it more difficult to send young people to prison.'

Again he struck a note of optimism: 'There has been some return of hope in the last year or two and an increasing willingness among prison staff to prepare prisoners for release and help them with their problems.' The word 'rehabilitation', however, should be avoided. 'Counselling and preparation for release are better words. The prison system has hit rock bottom at the moment and things can only improve. If overcrowding is reduced in the 1990s, there will be more time to deal with people as individuals, and with people who have special problems.'

He was under no illusion about the benefits of imprisonment. A person at liberty is more likely to respond to treatment; prison is much more likely to do harm than good. But prisons could be much more helpful than they are now. 'We need smaller prisons or smaller units, with well-trained staff and a low turnover of staff. Until now, training has concentrated on security and control. Prisoners should be as near as possible to their own homes. Prison staff want conspicuous leadership. This is not possible in the civil service machine. On balance, there should be moves towards agency status for the Prison Service. Certainly, there should be an identifiable leader of the Prison Service.'

I asked Stephen Shaw, as I had asked Peter Timms, about the statement of purpose of the prison system embodied in the notice now being displayed in all prisons where staff and prisoners meet:

Her Majesty's Prison Service serves the public by keeping in custody those committed by the courts. Our duty is to look after them with humanity and to help them lead law-abiding and useful lives in custody and after release.

'I welcome it,' he said, 'but I dislike the term "statement of purpose". There is a moral distinction between the purpose of imprisonment, which is containment for the protection of the public, and the ethos by which individual prisons should be run.' And he considered that the statement should include a number of additional elements, namely:

- Acknowledge the responsibility of the Prison Service to respect prisoners' rights;
- Spell out the role of the Prison Service in meeting prisoners' special needs;
- Establish the responsibility to provide a service for prisoners' relatives and friends;
- Acknowledge the role of the Prison Service in challenging the attitudes and behaviour which lead to offending;
- Uphold the preservation of links between prisoners and the community at large.

Stephen Shaw feels that the distinction between purpose and ethos has become blurred in the minds of the public. The purpose of imprisonment is to punish malefactors, but this does not mean that prisons have to be run in a punitive way.

Harry Fletcher

As the Assistant General Secretary of the National Association of Probation Officers, Harry Fletcher is responsible for relations with the press and Parliament and for campaigning. From 1976 to 1983, he was Senior Social Worker at the National Council for One Parent Families, responsible for casework and campaigning.

The Probation Service holds the key to the whole future of penal reform. The government proposals for punishment in the community, which I have consistently supported in principle, depend for their success on a full measure of cooperation from it.

Not long before I interviewed Harry Fletcher, the Probation Service had made their own views of their position abundantly plain. They had published an important document, *A Service under Threat – The Future of Probation*, in which they pointed out that in 1988 the Probation Service prepared 278,000 reports for courts and parole boards and, at the end of that year, 146,000 people were receiving probation supervision. The document continued: 'It costs the taxpayer £18 per week to supervise an offender in the community. Last year the average cost of keeping a person in prison was £275 per week. The record of the Probation Service is one of solid achievement with a long history of successfully supervising serious, high-risk offenders in the community, without compromising public safety and at a substantially lower cost than imprisonment.'

However, they now consider themselves to be a service under attack from some sections of the government and the Home Office.

The Probation Service, it is said, is confused about its role and accountability; it lacks a sense of direction and has not targeted its efforts sufficiently; it is reluctant to accept the need for change and slow to respond to new demands and develop systems to monitor its effectiveness; and the quality of its management is poor. From these criticisms come radical proposals to introduce a punitive community supervision order, to effect house arrest through electronic surveillance, to contract out existing areas of Probation Service work to the voluntary or commercial sector and to reorganize the service by abandoning its local roots in favour of a centrally administered agency. The effect of these changes would be to restrict constructive work with offenders and they would lead to a high level of breaches because of failure to meet the multiple and purposeless demands of supervision. This in turn would contribute to an increase, not a decrease, in the prison population.

Harry Fletcher began our conversation with some objective comments: 'The aims of the Probation Service have changed over the last decade. Prior to 1971 probation officers had a Home Office training, but since then it has been mandatory to have a social work qualification. The traditional aims of the service were to advise, assist and befriend, but this is now too narrow. Today the aims are: 1) To confront offenders with the effects of their offences; 2) To supervise in the community with the object of preventing further offences; and 3) To attempt to help the offender to restructure his life.'

The Probation Service needed to become more sophisticated and the number of offenders with previous custodial experience put on probation should be increased in dialogue with the courts. Harry Fletcher thought that it was unrealistic to think that the service could simply offer more of the same and expect those who sentence to use traditional probation. A *constructive package* should be offered to the court. For example, a burglar should attend a group with other burglars, psychologists and perhaps victims, to discuss the reasons for and effects of the offences, and to develop ways of restructuring their lives.

Management also had to become more sophisticated. At the moment there were inexpert selection procedures and poor ongoing training. Very few probation officers had the opportunity to acquire management skills as they came up through the ranks.

'The service,' Harry Fletcher continued, 'must make these constructive packages attractive to both ethnic minorities and women, and it must look into child-care provision for women offenders. In Holloway prison, two-thirds of the inmates have dependent children. Most of these women have committed acquisitorial cffences and are non-violent. There is great potential for emptying women's prisons. The service must develop female supervision with child care as a priority and no heavy labour.'

Harry Fletcher had good things and bad things to say about the government White Paper *Crime, Justice and Protecting the Public*. The aims and objectives were good, he felt, but the methods were wrong: 'We do not need a new order of the court more punitive than the existing one, and there should be greater consistency in sentencing.' The judiciary seem to him to be isolated and out of touch. Community service is admittedly punishment, but the experience should be constructive. 'The government want probation and community service to be much more punitive than they are at the moment, but this kind of punishment will prove effective only if the offender himself thinks it is useful.'

My talk with Harry Fletcher led me for the first time to realize that the words 'punishment' and 'punitive' have different connotations. Everyone must agree that community service is punishment. No one would want it to be punitive. The key question is whether the treatment, even if it benefits the community, is designed to benefit the offender.

Harry Fletcher was somewhat scathing about senior judges. 'They are all reactionaries, though the circuit judges and recorders are less isolated. Certain categories of offence should become not imprisonable, for example minor theft. It should be made difficult for magistrates to imprison.'

He was entirely in favour of a Sentencing Council. It should be responsible to the Lord Chancellor, who would give guidance to the judges. He returned, however, to his view that judges were reactionary. He implied that they would need a good deal of education before they gave effect to progressive guidelines.

As regards the reorganization of the Probation Service, Harry Fletcher referred to a 'deep suspicion of the Home Office which wants to control the service and make it tougher'. It was, however, difficult to justify the present structure with its blatant inconsistencies. There should be a national Probation Service with independent financial control. 'The Probation Service,' he told me, 'has a crucial role to play in prisons as trainers of prison officers in welfare work.' There are tensions, but probation officers play an increasing role. Prison officers are taking on some of the welfare work and probation officers are concentrating on counselling and emotional difficulties. For example, in prisons in the Southeast and in Liverpool, probation officers have been running trauma groups for prisoners who were transferred from Strangeways after the riot.

The caring ideal could be transferred to prisons. 'Rehabilitation had never really been tried.' I was well aware before I talked to Harry Fletcher that the success of the new government initiatives would depend on the cooperation of the Probation Service. Men like him are as necessary within the official world as in the world of probation. Too much harm has been done because the various interest groups will not talk to one another. Only good can come from greater mutual understanding.

Eric McGraw

Eric McGraw has been Director of the New Bridge for Ex-Prisoners for the past two years. He had previously gained worldwide experience as a United Nations consultant on population concerns. Before that he was a teacher. As mentioned earlier, I myself took the initiative in the setting-up of the New Bridge in 1955, much assisted by friends. At that time, I was finishing an inquiry into the causes of crime for the Nuffield Foundation and had visited a great many prisons and Borstals. I had become obsessed with the idea of helping the ex-prisoner 'to feel like a human being again, to help him or her to find the courage and the will to forge a new life for himself'.

I began by asking Eric McGraw: 'After thirty-four years, what would you say the New Bridge stands for today?' He waxed eloquent in reply. I must extract two passages from his answer:

First, the befriending service: 'We believe that for many prison inmates a prerequisite for the establishment of a trusting relationship is a prison visitor who is, and is seen to be, independent of the prison establishment. We provide support when requested to do so, following a prisoner's release.'

Second, the employment service: The New Bridge job-finding service is based on a 'one to one' interview, an approach preferred by many clients. This service provides an alternative to the employment services offered by both NACRO (National Association for the Care and Resettlement of Offenders) and the Apex Trust, who are primarily involved in Youth Training Schemes run on behalf of the government. They often exclude those who are not suitable for training or do not wish to participate in a training course.

It will be noticed that the emphasis has shifted a good deal from the initial concentration on befriending the ex-prisoner. That is still undertaken, but it is considered today that preparation for release should begin the moment a man enters prison. The work of the voluntary associates of the New Bridge in prison visiting is something that was not envisaged in the first instance but has become highly effective.

I listened carefully while Eric McGraw distinguished between the role of voluntary associates, such as those of the New Bridge, and official prison visitors.

'The prison visitor is usually a member of the National Association of Prison Visitors.

'He is appointed by the prison.

'He serves at one specified establishment.

'He receives support and advice, but no training.

'He is allocated by the prison to several inmates.

'He visits inmates usually on a prison wing or in an inmate's cell.

'And he is required to record each visit and provide any comments for the attention of the Governor.

'Our voluntary associates, on the other hand, consider it important to visit prisoners at the regular visiting times. Although from our point of view it might be better if they could meet in a private room, prisoners do prefer to be in a room with other people.'

The New Bridge struggles on, making slow but steady progress. When we began, we were viewed with suspicion by the Home Office. For various reasons, they persuaded themselves, it seems, that we were 'a homosexual society, primarily concerned with homosexuals'. When it was put to them that at the time I had eight children, they are supposed to have airily replied: 'Oh, that's just cover.' For many years now, the Home Office have recognized our work and provided a subsidy to cover about a fifth of our costs. In view of comparable subsidies elsewhere, this would seem to be a totally insufficient amount of assistance. Perhaps by the time these words are published, it will have been improved upon.

The New Bridge provides help to hundreds of people a year through the befriending and aftercare services, but when we think of the numbers in prison, now approaching 50,000, we must agree with Eric McGraw that there is a huge shortfall which can be filled only by statutory action. If they were more generously assisted by the State, the voluntary bodies could do far more than they do now, but the absence of the necessary statutory action is almost as evident today as when we formed the New Bridge thirty-five years ago.

Edward Fitzgerald

Edward Fitzgerald is a barrister who practises at the Criminal Bar and is especially concerned with prisoners. He took a Double First at Oxford and is married to my eldest granddaughter.

Lord Longford:
At the present time, do you see any way of improving the position of mentally disturbed offenders? Is there any change in the law that you consider essential?

Edward Fitzgerald:
Well, one of the things that concerns me at present is the power of the judge to say that someone is mentally disordered and in need of treatment, but that he proposes to punish him.

LL:
Could that happen today?

EF:
It does still sometimes happen. For example, when there has been a verdict of diminished responsibility, the judge has discretion to say that the prisoner should go to prison and not to a mental hospital.

LL:
So the judge has the option. The defendant no remedy?

EF:
The Court of Appeal could intervene when a mentally disordered prisoner has been sent to prison, but it does not always do so. There was the case of the schizophrenic burglar where the Lord Chief Justice took the view that, although he was a schizophrenic, he was responsible for his actions. The psychiatric evidence in that case was that he was mentally disordered and in need of treatment. In that case, too, the Lord Chief Justice came up with his own intuition that this man was in need of punishment. The error here is that a judge has the discretionary power to substitute his own opinion for that of a psychiatrist, and there is no recourse to a jury.

LL: What ought to be done?

EF: The solution is to enable a prisoner to establish that he is mentally disordered and in need of treatment before a jury, at which point the judiciary should have no discretion. The only situation at present in which there is no discretion is after a finding of McNaughton insanity.

LL: Just to clear up a point about the jury –

EF: The defendant should have the right to elect for a jury, so that he could have the additional protection of one.

LL: You say that people ought to be able to establish that they need treatment. Can they be refused permission to go to hospital on the grounds that they would not *benefit*?

EF: The answer is that in strict law they should not be, but in practice they are. The legal test is whether treatment is likely to alleviate or prevent a deterioration in their condition – and the word 'alleviate' does not mean cure. The shorthand description of the legislative test as a 'treatability test' is misleading but it has come to dominate the thinking both by judges and by psychiatrists.

LL: Strictly speaking, people qualify under the law if their condition can be 'alleviated'?

EF: In practice, psychiatrists tend to interpret that to mean that someone is curable. But there is a notion that psychopathy is untreatable. Many people who used to be treated as psychopaths in hospital are therefore left to moulder in prison – arsonists and sex offenders, for example.

        At present the prisoner faces a double veto. The judge can veto hospitalization on grounds that imprisonment is more appropriate than detention in a mental hospital. The psychiatrist can veto it on grounds that he does not consider the person 'curable' or, worse, does not want to treat him. There should be a right for a prisoner at any stage – remand, on sentence and after sentence, while serving a term of imprisonment – to establish his mental disorder and need of treatment, and then to have the right to be treated in hospital rather than in prison.

LL: 'In need of treatment' is how you put it?

EF: Yes.

LL: Do you consider that more could be done under the existing law? How could it be altered?

EF: The greatest problem is the lack of openness in the decisions that affect the prisoner. You can be put on Rule 43 [solitary confinement] without reasons, denied parole without reasons. No reasons are given for the decisions that are taken. But the case law is developing to require the giving of more reasons.

LL: Should prisoners have more right of access?

EF: Here there has been positive change – the recognition of an absolute right of access to the courts is new. These are *procedural* rights. However when it comes to *substantive* rights, for example good conditions, contacts with the outside world, exercise – there the courts will not help except in extreme cases. Prisoners in young offenders' institutions who are of an age to require education are supposed to get fifteen hours' education a week. That rule is routinely ignored and many of the positive rights that prisoners ought to have, such as exercise, are often denied them.

The neglect of prisoners gives rise to a strong case for entrenching minimum human rights safeguards in a constitutional manner. Prisoners and mental patients have little voting strength and they cannot always look to the legislature for the protection they require. They need some third power to protect their rights. That is why all the significant changes over the last fifteen years have come about either from the English courts or the European Convention on Human Rights.

LL: What significant changes?

EF: First, the right to freedom from censorship of all a prisoner's correspondence. The introduction of the right to telephone out of prison was undoubtedly influenced by the European decisions under Article 8 of the Convention. Access to lawyers and the courts have both been conferred by decisions of the European Court and the English courts. In the old days, a prisoner used to have to ask the permission of the Home Secretary to sue the Home Secretary. It is not necessarily because European countries are more enlightened than England, but because the European Convention safeguards certain fundamental rights for all people, including prisoners.

Where Parliament is sovereign, the tendency is for pressure groups with some electoral muscle, such as the trades unions, to win rights for their constituency. But prisoners and mental patients do not have any electoral muscle, as they rely on a notion of fundamental safeguards through a judicial power. Once prisoners could go to court, they began to make the developments themselves because they were able to point out all the inconsistencies.

LL: Who should go to prison?

EF: The judges have far too much discretion, particularly magistrates. The best example of the successful use of parliamentary limits was the legislation vetoing the power to imprison prostitutes for soliciting which, at a stroke, meant that a whole category of offenders did not go to prison. It did not lead to any diminution in the deterrent power of the courts, but it removed a senseless use of imprisonment and at least helped to reduce the number of female offenders. They should prohibit imprisonment for shoplifting of any sort, and first-time burglars should never go inside. If prison for first-time burglars was removed, the prison population could be reduced by many thousands. Replace it with community service and compensation. That is an example of possible legislation, because one-sixth of the prison population is made up of burglars. Generally speaking, prison sentences for dishonesty should be reduced. The inroads should be made on non-violent offenders. The proposals in *Crime, Justice and Protecting the Public* simply requiring judges to give reasons before they send someone to prison will make no difference.

LL: How do you persuade judges not to send offenders to prison?

EF: You remove their discretion to send certain categories of offender to prison and you provide alternatives that the judiciary will regard as genuinely punitive.

LL: Do you support punishment in the community as a new objective?

EF: The answer is that it is the right approach. Community service has been successful; there is general support for its extension. The problem is to make it a real alternative rather than something where the people who would not have gone to prison in any event are given community service.

LL: What about maximum sentences?

EF: The evidence is that judges do not use the maximum anyway. They are totally misleading guides. We could certainly reduce the maxima across the board for all offences and get rid of the mandatory life sentence. There should be fixed-term sentences for everybody.

LL: What is your view of the Carlisle proposals for parole?

EF: It is acceptable in my view that people should not be released until they have completed one-half of their sentence. Where I object to Carlisle is in its proposal to discriminate in sentencing between different types of offender. All prisoners should be entitled to release after completion of one-half of their sentence, subject to a postponement if they are convicted of disciplinary offences.

LL: What of the heavier end of sentencing?

EF: The discretionary life sentence has caused a lot of injustice. In my view it is based on a confusion of the notion of preventive detention, which is appropriate in a mental hospital setting, with the notion of imprisonment, which should be limited by principles of proportionality. Those who get discretionary life sentences now should have either fixed-term sentences or indeterminate detention in the mental hospital system, if they qualify.

LL: What would be your maximum sentence?

EF: Ideally, I would like a system in which the maximum was thirty years. It may be that in cases of serial killers you would have to allow for some increase. But I think there should be an absolute ceiling. One could envisage appalling conditions in which a serial killer who did not establish mental disorder could merit a sentence of forty or fifty years. Assuming their entitlement to remission, they could be out in twenty or twenty-five years.

LL: What do you feel about government emphasis on 'just deserts'?

EF: It is the only way you can make sense of a penal system. You must have some notion of proportionality. The argument then becomes: what kind of just deserts it is humane to impose? Within the context of sentencing, where outer limits are determined by proportionality, there is great scope for the rehabilitation and reform of offenders. Much more could be done to provide education and preparation for a prisoner's return to the community.

LL: Is there anything else you would like to say?

EF: I would like to have said more about how attempts to reform offenders while they are in prison could be integrated into the prison system. I would also like to have dealt with the need to use more non-custodial alternatives for mentally disordered offenders, such as psychiatric protection orders and guardianship orders. These confer quite extensive paternalistic powers and can be *effective* in providing compulsory treatment and control in the community, without taking up space in hospital.

LL: What exactly are you suggesting about constitutional safeguards for prisoners? Is it necessary to go as far as a written constitution to provide the safeguards you are advocating?

EF: It would be sufficient to incorporate the European Convention on Human Rights into English law. Then a prisoner or mental patient would have the right to go to court and (1) Challenge any inhumane conditions under Article 3 of the Convention which prohibits the inhumane and degrading treatment of all prisoners; (2) Challenge certain restrictions on his enjoyment of family life under Article 8; and (3) under Article 6 challenge the restriction on his letters to a lawyer or on his right to read and discuss what he wants as an unnecessary interference with his freedom of thought and expression.

Christopher Holtom

Christopher Holtom, who is a retired university lecturer, is the co-founder of a Victim Support Scheme which has subsequently served as the prototype for Victim Support Schemes all over the British Isles. He has also been a Borstal housemaster and has trained probation officers. He is now Vice-President of the National Association of Victim Support Schemes.

Lord Longford:	You started up the first Victim Support Scheme in 1973 in Bristol. Was that indeed the first one in Britain?
Christopher Holtom:	I was the first Chairman of the national organization and am now Vice-President.
LL:	You emphasize that no one is entitled to speak for all Victims' Schemes, but I feel that if anyone is entitled to speak for them it is you. Have you yourself ever been a victim?
CH:	Years ago I had the misfortune to have my overcoat stolen – when you needed clothing coupons to buy a new one – but otherwise, no.
LL:	So it was not personal experience that led you to take the matter up?
CH:	I was much involved with the National Association for the Care and Resettlement of Offenders locally in Bristol. We were surprised at the general lack of support and the amount of resistance we were receiving from the public. We came to the conclusion eventually that nothing was known about victims of crime and so we set up a study group. We got together members of the police, lawyers, magistrates and members of the prison service, as well as some ex-prisoners we had been working with, and then asked ourselves: How do we get in touch with victims?

LL: Very important point.

CH: We found them by reading local newspaper reports and approaching them.

LL: No doubt they didn't want to show up collectively – too often they regard themselves as an object of contempt.

CH: We found when we visited them that they felt isolated within the community – other people did not want to know. We found, too, that it was a bit like someone who had had a serious operation – it is upsetting to talk about it. Linked with that was a sense of guilt, that it was somehow their own fault that it had happened.

In the United States, there are a number of organizations who do campaign on behalf of victims and who say that the victim has a right to determine the punishment of the offender, which we would think not at all a good idea. The judge should be aware of the implications of the offence, but that doesn't mean to say that the victim should have a say in what the punishment of the offender should be.

LL: You say that from the beginning your organization has taken the line that it is not appropriate for victims to have a say in the punishment of offenders –

CH: It would be too unpredictable and courts are not equipped for that sort of thing.

LL: Would you say that no attention at all should be paid by the courts to the situation of the victim when the offender is sentenced?

CH: That depends on the crime. When it is a question of rape, where there is a terrible fear of the offender on the part of the victim, I think it is appropriate that the victim should be informed when the offender is to be released. The parole supervising officer should certainly have in mind some control over the offender to prevent him from meeting the victim. There have been cases where a victim has come face to face in the street with an offender. We are not saying that the victim should determine whether he gets parole, but should be made aware of the decision.

LL: Should the court go further and say where the prisoner is going to live?

CH: Particularly where incest is concerned, yes. The law requires the offender not to be in the same household. Either the child is taken into care or the offender is prevented from living there. One should still be aware when the crime is of a one-off character but has repercussions in the shape of fear for a long time in the lives of victims.

LL: You are saying that the actual decision as to where the offender lives is made known to the victim?

CH: I am not saying that that applies in all cases by any means . . .

LL: Are you speaking throughout this interview in your official capacity?

CH: I am speaking as Christopher Holtom on the basis of my experience.

LL: Do you represent the views of the National Association of Victim Support Schemes?

CH: We have given evidence to a Select Committee on this, and that is the line we took.

LL: Are there any organizations outside your umbrella? You don't represent all victims. Are there other organizations?

CH: There are about half a dozen who have decided not to affiliate to the National Association for various reasons.

LL: Talking of organizations: would it be right to say that, as an organization, you have deliberately declined to offer opinions on appropriate sentences?

CH: The question we ask is whether or not the offender should make some sort of restitution to the victim – there should be a balance between fines and restitution. Fines, unfortunately, are the perquisite of the court – restitution could benefit the victim. But the regulations have changed and courts are now empowered to give priority to restitution over fines as compensation for emotional damage.

LL: Would you say that the relatives of victims, for example, ought to be awarded compensation whether or not they suffer permanent loss?

CH: At the moment, funds from the Criminal Injuries Compensation Board are available only for physical harm, and only to the actual victim. There may, however, sometimes be an additional payment taking into account emotional pain but, as I understand it, only if there is physical injury. My own *personal* view is that we should recognize the emotional hurt caused by a non-violent offence as well. The State has a duty to the citizen to protect him and owes a duty to recompense him for the failure to protect him from crime.

LL: The Criminal Injuries Compensation Board at present only recompense in the case of violent offences? Is that enough?

CH: The arrangements should be extended to cover offences causing emotional hurt as well as physical harm. Some people who have been burgled suffer very considerably afterwards. The way I look at it is that the outside world may be a dangerous place, but when you have been burgled your feeling of security in your own home has been invaded.

LL: As far as the law is concerned, would you extend compensation to cover all injuries?

CH: The Criminal Injuries Compensation Board has fairly recently introduced a minimum below which they will not pay anything, but we feel that a symbolic gesture by the State in recompensing victims helps to cover emotional hurt.

LL: You criticize this decision of the government?

CH: Well, the system was getting overloaded; there was an immense backlog of claimants.

LL: At any rate your organization is strongly critical of this new minimum level? What about government funding. Do you think the government should increase the National Association's grant?

CH: I have felt for a very long time that the State has ignored the plight of victims, but now they are giving financial support to our work. We would not wish to be totally funded by government.

LL: But you would still like to have more?

CH: It is healthy to have to go to other sources.

LL: But more would be acceptable, although not to the point where you lost your independence? I think the government should pay out more to victims. Do you think the government should pay when the criminals can't?

CH: I would like to see something like National Health Insurance – say, a National Crime Insurance. I emphasize that this is a personal view. I would like to see a situation where you could claim as a right when you become a victim of crime. My feeling is that the State has a responsibility for the extent of crime – they have taken it on themselves and they have failed to protect. This is a personal view.

LL: What do you see happening in the next few years? What will be the thrust of your main effort nationally?

CH: There are a number of areas where we have not been able to do as much as we could. We have a number of projects in mind, for example children within families. We need to explore the effect on a child where there has been a burglary. We have a special project on the effect on relatives of murder victims. Then there is the way in which we could improve the situation in courts. There are several levels here: one is the extent to which the system tends to take victims for granted. They are made to wait in the main waiting-room alongside the offender and can be intimidated as a result.

LL: Do you think they could be kept separate?

CH: This is actually happening. One or two courts have already begun to do this. But, when a victim gets into court, the way in which the court deals with you can also be an unhappy experience. You can be subjected to aggressive cross-examination.

LL: How do you protect the victim?

CH: We maintain that it is the duty of the judge or magistrate to intervene if they feel the cross-examination is not appropriate. In rape cases, for example, the victim feels that she is being accused. Another thing is that, as the law stands at the moment, the defence can make a plea of mitigation which cannot be challenged. Unscrupulous claims made in the plea of mitigation can imply that the victim was partly to blame – and the victim has no right of reply.

LL: I can see how that could be damaging to the victim. Would you say that it should be possible to challenge such pleas of mitigation?

CH: Yes, if there is a factual error. The offender may have told his lawyer that such and such happened which did not in fact happen, and the victim can challenge and say it was not like that. Not only talking of rape cases, but also of assault cases – the victim can often be made to feel that he or she is to blame.

LL: Victim Support Schemes have been very successful in establishing themselves. What do you feel they can achieve and are achieving?

CH: We have provided help to a large number of victims – last year to about 7000 in all – 600 or 700 a month. At headquarters we employ one or two people, but we have a group of volunteers who do the actual work.

LL: When you say 'help', what does that involve? You don't provide victims with financial help?

CH: We provide emotional help, factual advice on where to get help with claiming benefits, help in claiming insurance if someone has been burgled – and if they are insured, of course. We don't wait for people to come to us, we go to them. We reckon that the victim after the experience is often too shocked – they are not capable of taking a decision for themselves to seek help. The police give us the names of victims and we send a volunteer to visit them.

LL: Do most people like a visit?

CH: This was interesting – because when we started we expected complaints about invasion of privacy, which in the event happened only seldom. People would say: 'We don't need any help, but thanks for asking us.' It made them feel that at least the community was concerned.

LL: But with all your experience after all these years, are victims still reluctant to come forward on their own?

CH: When a person is in shock, they are not normally able to reach sensible decisions.

LL: Is there still the 'British stiff upper lip'?

CH: Still a bit of it.

LL: There is so much talk of doing a lot more for victims. The government were not at all ready in 1979, but your organization has changed all that.

CH: We now find that the Home Office and the Lord Chief Justice take us seriously and listen to what we have to say. They see us as a source of information as to victims' needs.

LL: It has not been an election winner. If you take your own organization, for example, are victims represented on it?

CH: Not as such. We don't seek them out as victims. This may be a fault. The management for such a scheme should be made up of people who have some kind of positive contribution to make to the work. We say we want somebody from the police, somebody from probation and the other services, and so on. The reason is that we maintain that being a victim is not a status but an experience. We hope to get people who have suffered in that way to become ordinary citizens again.

LL: You don't want people to become permanent victims?

CH: If you made a study of our volunteers, you would probably find that some of them have been victims but that their motivation in joining the scheme is that they are anxious to help others.

LL: The strongest motivation is that you become aware of the need and the possibility of helping. The work is almost a reward in itself. Coming back to the criminals – do you make any attempt to bring victims and criminals together?

CH: Not as an organization. There are two things here: we do not want, as it were, to dilute our efforts with victims and we are anxious lest we should, so to speak, victimize the victim a second time by putting him or her in a situation which could be stressful. There are a number of different people trying to get things going in various places. We have been involved in discussion, but we have not linked ourselves as an organization with them. We thought it might be misunderstood and divert our efforts. We are sympathetic but cautious too – seeing it would be good for the offender, but may lead to inappropriate pressure on the victim to cooperate.

LL: Do you wish to say anything yourself about punishment? And how to treat criminals? Nationally and locally your organization does not express views. You have so much knowledge and you are not making it available.

CH: Victims are very different in their attitude. Some are very vengeful, some are sympathetic. Who are we, as an organization, to speak for them?

LL: I do see that.

CH: The position is not likely to alter.

LL: Have you got your own views on punishment?

CH: It is a 'Yes, but . . .'. What I did not mention was that I started my 'criminal' career in the prison service, as a Borstal housemaster. My professional training was in probation and I have trained ordinary workers and special probation officers. I am still active in BACRO (Bristol Association for the Care and Resettlement of Offenders).

On punishment: the thing that is clear to me is that punishment does not solve anything, in the sense that it does not change behaviour. I am also aware that there is a very real need for people to be punished. It is an understandable feeling in the community that people should be punished if they break the law. Some action should be taken to mark disapproval if they misbehave. People are not to be free to continue to burgle without anything being done to prevent their doing so. 'Target hardening' is the answer – making it more difficult for them to break in.

I always remember when I first went into the prison service. I was told: 'Men are sent to prison as a punishment – and not for punishment.'

LL: I sympathize with the government's latest idea of punishment in the community. The Probation Service do not like it. But I do think you are quite right – people should be penalized, but need not be sent to prison. If they are going to be dealt with outside, it really can be punishment. Community service is punishment. I have recently realized that there is a large difference between inflicting punishment and being punished.

CH: I am talking about penalties. There is a price to be paid, but what the price is and whether it should be hurtful is another matter. I don't see any particular value in hurting people. Hurting people is seldom constructive.

LL: Do you call denying freedom hurtful?

CH: It is in order to get people to face the situation. They have to be held in order to face it.

LL: But how often can we convince them that it is for their own good?

A Joint Manifesto for Penal Reform

I cannot conclude the evidence from penal reformers without referring to an important document. In February 1989, a number of the leading organizations dedicated to penal reform issued what they called *A Joint Manifesto for Penal Reform*.

Their programme falls into two main sections. The first is concerned with reducing imprisonment and the second with improving prison conditions and prisoners' rights. I will pick out a few items, several of which have been discussed by our witnesses. Under the heading 'Guidelines for Imprisonment', for example, the manifesto lays down that:

- Statutory restrictions on the use of imprisonment for adults should be introduced, similar to those in the 1982 Criminal Justice Act restricting the use of custody for young offenders.

- The use of custody for non-violent offences should be reduced by sentencing guidelines, drawn up by a Sentencing Council and issued as practical directions by the Lord Chief Justice. These should set ceilings for different types of offence, detail the amount of weight to be attached to such factors as age, previous convictions and so on; and emphasize the need to make repeated use of non-custodial sentences for repeated minor offences.

Maximum penalties should be reduced. Life imprisonment should be the maximum and not the mandatory penalty for murder. Bail should become much more readily available. Juveniles should no longer be held on remand or under sentence within the prison system.

Under the heading of 'Prison Conditions and Prisoners' Rights', they insist that:

- A code of minimum standards for penal establishments should be introduced, with a timetable for achieving it. The code should set norms for acceptable living conditions and guarantee access to work and education. Resources should be diverted from the current massive expansion of the prison system to bring existing prisons up to the standard laid down by the code.

- Crown immunity should be lifted from prisons.

- Censorship of letters and restrictions on their number should be ended for all but Category A prisoners and those on the escape list; access to telephones should be extended to all prisoners; and visiting rights and entitlement to home leave should be increased.

- A Prisons Ombudsman should be established.

- The prison disciplinary system should be reorganized along the lines of the recommendations of the Committee on the Prison Disciplinary System under the chairmanship of Mr Peter Prior which reported in 1985. Independent Prison Disciplinary Tribunals should replace Boards of Visitors as the upper adjudicatory tier.

On parole the manifesto is divided, but on resettlement it lays down that 'There should be a substantial increase in the number of aftercare hostels, training schemes and other resettlement facilities for offenders in the community.'

I am myself broadly in favour of the manifesto. Certainly if its findings were implemented, prisons would be better places than they are now. Before examining the issues in detail, however, such as sentencing policy, let us hear from some witnesses who have much to tell us about the prison experience itself.

III

The Punished

The Guildford Four and the Maguire Family Group

Nearly all prisoners are punished because they have broken the law. The law may be a bad one and so may the sentence, but the fact of breaking the law is common to nearly all prisoners. To nearly all, but not to all. Every now and then there is a miscarriage of justice. There have been some notable cases in Britain in recent times, some of them exposed by the indomitable Ludovic Kennedy. The 'Birmingham Six' have always been innocent in the eyes of the present writer. By the time this book appears, that innocence will, I hope, have been legally established.

At the moment I will concentrate on one case only: that of the Guildford Four and the Maguire Family Group. I will sum it up in the words of Robert Kee who, with the solicitor Alistair Logan from the beginning, and with Cardinal Hume later on, has led the fight to see that truth and justice should prevail:

> The specific proposition to be faced is that in sentencing four people to life imprisonment for the IRA murders at Guildford in 1974, and in sentencing seven other people to long terms of imprisonment on a charge which derived from those Guildford murders, of possessing nitro-glycerine unlawfully, British courts, just over ten years ago, were responsible for a miscarriage of justice on a scale unprecedented in Britain in this century.

The horror of the outrage for which these eleven persons were unjustly convicted should not be played down. On 5 October 1974, five people were killed and some sixty injured in the bombing of two public houses in Guildford. On 7 November of the same year, the bombing of a public house in Woolwich resulted in two deaths. Heavy penalties had to be exacted, provided that the real culprits could be caught.

The opposite occurred in this case. Those convicted of the Guildford murders were Carole Richardson, by then aged eighteen; Patrick Armstrong, aged twenty-five; Paul Hill, aged twenty-one; and Gerard Conlon, aged twenty-one. Another seven persons were convicted of 'unlawfully possessing nitro-glycerine'. In fact, they were accused of running a bomb factory – a ludicrous charge, as anyone who has looked into the case has long since recognized. It is almost incredible that Patrick Maguire, aged thirteen at the time of his arrest, should have been given a sentence of three years which he spent in a young person's prison; in the company, that is to say, of young delinquents up to the age of twenty-one.

All that arose from the events of 1974. On the morning of 19 October 1989, Mr Roy Amlot QC, on behalf of the Director of Public Prosecutions, rose at the Old Bailey before the Lord Chief Justice and two other lords of appeal. He revealed that the 'confessions' to the crimes – the only evidence there had ever been against the Guildford Four – were the product of fabrications on the part of the Surrey Constabulary of the day. The Four were set free that afternoon.

Game, set and match to the champions of justice? By no means yet. In July 1990, Sir John May, who was appointed to inquire into the convictions of the Guildford Four and the Maguire Family Group, delivered an interim report. His conclusions were uncompromising:

> Having regard to all these matters it is quite clear to me that I should recommend that the Home Secretary should refer the case of the Maguire Seven to the Court of Appeal.

The Maguire Family Group are still living under a horrible slur. Until that slur is removed by the Court of Appeal, there can be no question of justice being done. Mrs Anne Maguire, the supposed 'mother' of the bomb factory (though she has no idea how to make a bomb), served nine years of a fourteen-year sentence, the others varying amounts. Giuseppe Conlon, the father of Gerard Conlon, one of the Guildford Four, died in prison. When I met him he was already a dying man and I was convinced of his innocence. What was vastly more important, however, was that Cardinal Hume paid a pastoral visit to him in prison and came away convinced not only of his innocence but of the innocence of all the convicted persons.

In May 1985, Gerry Fitt (now Lord Fitt of Bell's Hill), who had fought like a tiger for the Maguires, initiated a debate in the House of Lords. He began by quoting Anne-Marie Maguire, who had been nine at the time of the arrests:

My family, my father and my mother have all been convicted. A lot of years out of their lives have been taken away from them for no reason at all. Nothing will ever fill the gap that we have lost between each other. And if the truth does not come out while my Mum and Dad are still alive, then I hope that one day I will have children and my brothers will have children, and they will keep continuing in this campaign until the total innocence of my family has been proved once and for all.

I myself met Mrs Anne Maguire more than once while she was serving her sentence. She was strong then in asserting her innocence. She is stronger than ever today, now that over two hundred Members of Parliament have signed a statement asserting it. She must not be misunderstood: suffering, particularly unjustified suffering, can never in itself be good, but it can be accepted in a spirit that strengthens the sufferer. This has certainly been the case with Anne Maguire, who has been fighting heroically not only for herself but for her whole family.

While I was writing this book, she came to see me at the House of Lords, bringing with her her son Patrick, now aged twenty-nine. I am sure that he was telling the truth when he described how the police had beaten him at the time of his arrest. Anne Maguire has told me that she herself was knocked about. Since Patrick came out of prison twelve years ago, the whole experience has continued to haunt him. He has never been able to settle down to a regular job, though he leads a respectable life. I hope and pray that when the cloud of unjust conviction is lifted, he and the rest of his family will be able to face life on normal terms.

But, it will be asked, how on earth could the Maguire family have been implicated in all this? The answer is somewhat bizarre. Under intense pressure from the police, two of the Guildford Four, Paul Hill and Gerard Conlon (Anne Maguire's nephew), in addition to confessing their own involvement, incriminated the

Maguires in the running of a bomb factory. The police, not unnaturally, followed up this clue intensively and gleefully announced that traces of nitro-glycerine had been found on the hands or, in the case of Anne Maguire on the glove, of the Maguires.

There was much scientific argument as to whether the nitro-glycerine could have necessarily indicated an explosive subject. One would have thought that at least a reasonable doubt existed. But with the convictions of the Guildford Four no doubt fresh in their minds, the jury convicted all seven of the group. Sir John May's interim report deals with the scientific evidence in painstaking detail, but his conclusions are stark:

In my opinion it has been shown that the whole scientific basis upon which the prosecution was founded was in truth so vitiated that on this basis alone the Court of Appeal should be invited to set aside the convictions.

Sir John May goes on to remark of the trial itself:

The conduct of the trial can be challenged on at least the two points to which I have earlier referred. I do not think that the jury were adequately directed about the effect of Exhibit 60 on the foundation of the Crown's case, namely the exclusivity of the TLC/toluene test for NG [nitro-glycerine]. In addition, in my opinion Mr Higgs' evidence about the negative results of the tests on the 916 hand test kits was inadmissible [Mr Higgs was a scientist called as an expert witness].

For the Guildford Four, the question of compensation (and compensation has been accepted in principle) is being fought out. Here again, however, it is impossible to believe that the full truth has yet emerged. It was fortunate that the Surrey police did not destroy the written evidence of their fabrications, but no one can shut their eyes to the fact that extraordinary confessions were obtained by extraordinary means, including the reference to the Maguires. Whatever the precise details of the pressure applied, it is clear that it was illegal and utterly immoral.

What can be done to prevent such a grave miscarriage of justice in future? The judiciary come out of the affair very badly and the Home Office ministers not at all well. The Court of Appeal set aside almost with contempt in 1977 the admissions of the IRA's Balcombe Street bombers that they had carried out the Guildford and Woolwich bombings, and that they knew nothing of the Guildford Four. It needed Cardinal Hume, two law lords and two former Home Secretaries to induce the Home Secretary of the day to set up the investigation which ultimately led to the discovery of the crucial evidence.

As I correct the proofs of this book (December 1990), the issues involved are still being investigated and the Maguire Family Group await the verdict of the Court of Appeal. One thing at least is clear already: some new form of investigatory machinery, independent of the police and the judiciary, must be established to deal with cases of this kind. In the meantime, the struggle to secure justice for the Maguires continues unremittingly.

Chris Tchaikovsky

Chris Tchaikovsky – tall, slim, a late graduate of Essex University and forty-five years of age (though she looks much less) – is a very remarkable woman. I have never met anyone with a career like hers. Coming from a rich family and a rebel from her schooldays, she took to crime (mainly fraud) at the age of seventeen and practised it for thirteen years with considerable financial success.

In a chapter in *Criminal Women* (1985), she describes her motivation as it seemed to her at the time of her final sentence:

> I was thoroughly sick of the continuous criminal cry that it was all because of one's upbringing or lack of education, or mental instability. We were personable, intelligent and had as much going for us as anyone. Why should we pretend to be some kind of inadequates? I refused to identify with disadvantaged losers in the social lottery. I had travelled as much as I had wanted, and I had experienced more excitement than most. I had enjoyed both the dangers and the rewards, and my criminality was the result of a rational choice – nobody had coerced or cajoled me into it.

In later years she had been at great pains to explain and excuse the conduct of 'criminal women' by describing their backgrounds. She offers no such explanation or excuse in her own case.

Chris Tchaikovsky was bored and disenchanted with the criminal way of life by the time of her final arrest. But what sea change turned a selfish young woman into someone who is today a selfless and most effective labourer on behalf of others? Perhaps one day she will throw more light on the matter. For the moment, we can only turn to another passage from the book. In the last chapter, 'Women in Prison', by Pat Carlen (now Professor Carlen) and Chris Tchaikovsky, we read: 'It was because she was in prison at a time when a woman burned to death in her cell that Chris Tchaikovsky decided that she must begin a campaign to publicize the conditions in women's prisons.' The outcome has been the organization Women in Prison, a potent influence for penal reform not only among women. It goes from strength to strength under Chris Tchaikovsky's leadership and inspiration. To visit the offices is to be submerged in a flood of activists and media visitors of both sexes.

What follows is a summary of their philosophy and positive proposals.

Chris Tchaikovsky repudiated to me the title of feminist. 'I don't like that word any more. It has been spoilt for me by intolerant extremists. I prefer to describe us as representatives of the women's movement.'

It would be a mistake to suppose that Women in Prison are concerned only to improve the treatment of women. In a recent document they declare unequivocally their long-term aim: 'The daily experience of women in prison strengthens WIP's primary and most important objective – to see an end to prisons altogether.' Since at the time of writing there are over thirty times more men in prison than women, it is obvious that any successful campaign by Women in Prison will benefit more men than women, even if we bear in mind the wives and children of the male prisoners.

An appendix to *Criminal Women* sets out two lists of necessary reforms, each consisting of ten items. In the first, Women in Prison campaigning for women prisoners demand:

1. Improved safety conditions, particularly in Holloway prison where women have been burned to death in their cells.

2. The introduction of a range of facilities (e.g. more visits, including family and conjugal visits in relaxed surroundings, more association with other prisoners, fewer petty rules) aimed both at reducing tension and, subsequently, at the number of drugs prescribed for behaviour and mood control rather than the benefit of prisoners.

3. Improved, non-discriminatory and non-paternalistic education, job-related training, leisure and work facilities.

4. Improved training and supervision of prison officers, aimed at reducing their present discriminatory practices against women from ethnic minorities and lesbian, disabled or mentally or emotionally disturbed women.

5. A mandatory and non-discriminatory income-entitlement to meet the basic needs of women prisoners.

6. Improvement of the existing child-care facilities in prisons together with the introduction of a whole new range of child-care facilities for mothers receiving a custodial sentence (e.g. new centres specially for mothers and children; contacts with local nurseries and parents' groups).

7. Improved medical facilities in general and specialized facilities for women during pregnancy, childbirth and menstruation.

8. Dismantling of the punitive disciplinary structure coupled with the development of official recognition of prisoner participation in the organization of the prison.

9. Non-discriminatory sentencing of women.

10. Unrestricted access to the Boards of Visitors for representatives from women's organizations, community, ethnic minority and other minority (e.g. lesbian) organizations.

In the second list, Women in Prison campaigning for *all* prisoners demand:

1. Democratic control of the criminal justice and penal systems with: suspension of Official Secrets Act restrictions on the availability of information about prisons; public accountability of the Home Office Prison Department for its administration of the prisons; public inquiries replacing Home Office internal inquiries into the deaths of prisoners, injuries and complaints in general together with Legal Aid to enable prisoners' families to be represented at any such inquiry.

2. Reduction in the length of prison sentences.

3. Replacement of the parole system with the introduction of half-remission on all sentences. Access to a sentence-review panel after serving seven years of a life sentence.

4. Increased funding for non-custodial alternatives to prisons (e.g. community service facilities, sheltered housing, alcohol recovery units) together with greater use of the existing sentencing alternatives (e.g. deferred sentence, community service order, probation with a condition of psychiatric treatment etc.), with the aim of removing from prisons all who are there primarily because of drunkenness, drug dependency, mental, emotional or sexual problems, homelessness or inability to pay a fine.

5. Abolition of the censorship of prisoners' mail.

6. Abolition of the Prison Medical Service and its replacement by normal National Health Service provision coupled with abolition of the present system whereby prison officers vet, and have the power to refuse, prisoners' requests to see a doctor.

7. Provision of a law library in prisons so that prisoners may have access to information about their legal rights in relation to DHSS entitlement, employment, housing, marriage and divorce, child-custody, court proceedings, debt, prison rules etc.

8. Improved living and sanitary conditions together with a mandatory income entitlement to meet basic needs.

9. Non-discretionary rights to call witnesses and to full legal representation of prisoners at Visiting (internal) Court proceedings together with the abolition of the charge of 'making false and malicious allegations against an officer'.

10. A review of the existing methods of the recruitment and training of prison discipline staff.

In the first list some of the items can only refer to women, for example, items 6 and 7. Others depend on the assumption that women are treated worse in prison than men, of which more in a moment.

Are women, by virtue of their gender, likely to suffer more in prison than men? Baroness Blackstone, Master of Birkbeck College and a distinguished writer on penal reform, had this to say in an article in the *Observer*: 'Prison appears to have an especially destructive effect on women.' As I understand it, she means that women in prison should be treated more sensitively than men because they *are* more sensitive. Chris Tchaikovsky rejects such language with scorn. She would never agree with any suggestion from me, for example, that women should be regarded as intrinsically 'special'. On the contrary, so long as they are regarded as somehow 'different' in a male-dominated society, they will be treated worse. She certainly considers that they are treated worse at the moment.

It seems to be accepted that women are punished much more often than men in prison. Chris Tchaikovsky explains that easily enough. A higher standard of behaviour has come to be expected of women. 'If a woman uses a four-letter word, she is at once put on a charge. If a man uses one, no notice is taken.' This is offered as a small example of a widespread injustice. But to my masculine eye there is a certain incongruity when, for example, the important policy document *Breaking the Silence* (from the Women's Equality Group), which Chris helped to produce, demands that male prison officers should no longer be employed in women's prisons. Are women prison officers then to be excluded from male prisons where the vast majority of prisoners are housed? If so, the champions of equal opportunities might have something to say.

Chris Tchaikovsky argues that many women have suffered or been threatened with sexual abuse by men by the time they come to prison. True or false (and it must be true in some cases), that seems to put them in a special category. She would trust male governors and probation officers because of their professional training, and because they do not have a day-to-day controlling function on the landings, i.e. the living quarters of female prisoners. She insists, however, that women in prison should be allowed the choice of a male or female doctor in view of the special demands of intimacy. In general (and here, I think, she would say that she speaks for herself and not for the women's movement) she is against the sexual integration of prisons. To repeat the point, this would restrict opportunities for women in the same way as they were restricted at, for example, universities before sexual integration was embarked upon.

'Why are some 48,000 men in prison but only 1500 women?' I asked her. 'The view is often expressed, and not only by men, that men steal, for example, for the sake of their family.' Chris thought that there was an element of truth in this hypothesis. More fundamentally, she said, women have been conditioned by a male-dominated society into accepting a submissive role. This is not a desirable psychological state of being. In an age of true women's liberation, there would be none of this submissiveness.

In general, as a true daughter (or sister) of the women's movement, Chris is determined to resist and destroy the feminine stereotype. I asked her whether she would not agree that women were more self-sacrificing. She rejected that dangerous notion out of hand. Once such a notion was firmly established, as hitherto it has been to a large extent, a male-dominated society would make sure that women were called on for more than their share of sacrifice.

I asked her about lesbianism in prison. She told me, rather to my surprise, that there was very little sex in women's prisons. She agreed that emotional, that is to say loving, friendships abounded. We both seem happy to think that is so. Here, surely, it seems that women are superior to men whose training in keeping a stiff upper lip makes them more inhibited. But here again Chris refused to believe that the difference was intrinsic. Proper conditioning would get rid of the stiff upper lip along with other male inhibitions.

No one who has worked as a prison visitor or in penal reform for many years can fail to be profoundly grateful to Chris Tchaikovsky and Women in Prison for the passion and dedication that they have brought to bear on the attempt to improve all prisons. That does not mean that one has to share all their assumptions, however. I was told, for example, that 'chivalry is chauvinism'.

My feeble protest that I had never met a woman who was unhappy to walk out of a room before me was brushed aside. Many women with a very different standpoint from that of Chris Tchaikovsky have laboured in their own way, inside and outside, for male and female prisoners. But no one who cares for prisoners male and female can fail to salute the achievements, actual and potential, of Women in Prison.

Michael Bettsworth

Many educated men and women, before and after Oscar Wilde, have been humiliated, few more so than Michael Bettsworth. Until he went to prison, Michael's whole working life had been in teaching. Having taught at Winchester for some years, he founded an independent, coeducational boarding school for children between six and eighteen years of age. He was convicted of three sexual offences with a girl under the age of sixteen, for which the maximum sentence would have been six years. Given his position as headmaster, he considers that his sentence of eighteen months was lenient, all the more so as after six months he was out on parole. But he insists, and I believe him, that he was innocent, and must therefore be seen as a victim of maltreatment.

The worst thing, Michael told me during our interview, was waiting for his trial. 'You become a non-person, and it is the uncertainty that is so difficult to bear.' When it came to the trial, there were allegations relating to three dates over a six-week period. He insists that he had perfect alibis, but for whatever reason the jury decided against him. He started his sentence in Exeter prison, where he was put on Rule 43 (solitary confinement) and not allowed off it. This decision was no doubt intended to protect him from assault by other prisoners because he was a sex offender, but Michael was ready to take his chance. He gained the reputation of being a model prisoner.

At Leyhill, an open prison with an excellent reputation, he was placed in a dormitory with cubicles, and for a long time had a horrible experience. His trial had had a lot of publicity. He was persecuted, humiliated and branded a 'nonce'. He encountered the same sort of ostracism when working in the prison kitchen. On one occasion he hit a man who was abusing him, knocking him through a door. He was ignored at mealtimes. The only consolation, apart from visits from his devoted wife and children, were the many letters he received each week, all nice letters and many from his previous pupils. His school is still flourishing today.

Given his background and the offences for which he was

convicted, Michael's treatment in prison might be thought pre-
dictable. Much more surprising, however, are his feelings on the
attitude of the staff. 'Leyhill is an open prison, which is supposed
to be for people who can be trusted.' Yet, according to him, the
staff treated him discourteously. 'You were treated as untrust-
worthy at Leyhill. That was my experience.' On one occasion,
Michael told me, he was fined and given an enormous dressing-
down for not being at roll-call, when he was attending a course on
how to run a small business. The former headmaster reacted in a
way that is perhaps incomprehensible for those who have not
undergone his experience. He started systematically to evade the
rules and became an energetic smuggler.

Michael is very severe on Leyhill. I have visited Leyhill several
times over the years and thought it a relatively enlightened
prison, but I was judging it from the outside. At any rate, Judge
Tumim, the Chief Inspector of Prisons and a severe critic of much
else in the prison system, has singled out Leyhill for praise.
Michael could not think of anything constructive to say about the
place. He found no attempt being made to 'reform or rehabilitate'.

'Prison is always going to do more harm than good. It is no
deterrent. If it were a deterrent, there would be no recidivism.'
Michael is blunt, although he accepts that some people must go to
prison, violent people in the main. For someone like himself,
however, nothing was gained by incarcerating him. He was
ruined as soon as the rumours began to circulate about 'his affair
with a girl'. His trial and his conviction, he feels, were punishment
enough. 'If the object of prison is to reform and rehabilitate, then
those conditions must be created. In other words, treatment must
be provided which is totally unlike that now provided in prison.'

Michael accepts the concept of punishment in the community,
but not *humiliation* in the community. Any step to reduce the
numbers in prison would receive his sympathy. 'Too many people
go to prison and are made worse than they are already.' I asked
him, as a former headmaster, whether he accepted the necessity
for punishment in schools. He replied that he had always
punished children in their own interest. He acknowledged that
the threat of punishment had to be there. He once beat a boy 'who

had gone too far', but he was not offering that as an example to be followed.

When shown the transcript of our interview, Michael added a sad comment: 'I believe at bottom that the vast majority of the population are indifferent to the fate of wrongdoers.' His conclusions about prison can hardly be described as dispassionate, but nor are those of the representatives of the Establishment.

Rosie Johnston

Rosie Johnston is the daughter of an architect father and a novelist mother, Susanna, who accompanied her when I interviewed them after lunch in the House of Lords. Her grandfather, Sir Christopher Chancellor, was an eminent man, the Chairman of Reuters. Her uncles are well known in the literary and journalistic worlds.

On 5 December 1986, at Oxford Crown Court, Rosie was sentenced to nine months in prison for obtaining drugs for a friend, Olivia Channon. The daughter of a Cabinet minister and from a prominent family, Olivia had subsequently died from an accidental overdose of drugs and drink. The case aroused enormous interest which haunted Rosie right up to the moment of her release from prison. It is easy to believe, though this could never be proved, that the media interest helped to bring about what was surely a severe sentence.

She served that sentence in three prisons: Holloway, Bullwood Hall in Essex and East Sutton Park, an open prison in Kent. Rosie was not very long in Holloway and was sorry to be transferred. It is difficult to know from her striking book *Inside Out* (1990) whether she disliked Bullwood Hall or East Sutton Park more. Bullwood Hall was externally and internally extremely unattractive. East Sutton Park would seem to the outer eye a pleasant place, but like many other prisoners Rosie found life in a dormitory hard to bear. One wonders why dormitories are still the general rule in open prisons.

She has vividly described my own visits to her at Bullwood Hall. After I left on the first occasion, a fellow prisoner said to her: 'You must have done something pretty bad, Rosie, for that old nutter to come to see you.' Rosie's reply was robust – 'B----- off.' Throughout her ordeal she preserved, at whatever inner cost, a buoyant spirit.

Rosie   The judge in fact said: 'You have suffered greatly and
Johnston: I am deeply sorry for you. But I am sending you to
           prison for nine months.'

Lord Longford:	Susanna, what do you feel about the sentence?
Susanna Johnston:	My feelings about the method of sentencing are almost stronger than the sentence itself. The most horrifying aspect is the publicity – quite out of all proportion. The judge opened his speech by saying: 'My learned Counsel: You have *nearly* persuaded me . . . but not quite.' To me, with my limited experience of anything like that, it was one of the most horrifying sentences I have ever heard. That something so cruel could hang on the verbal ability of a lawyer – it was quite terrifying. Also in the case of this judge, it was absolutely clear that he had been swayed by the media. He spoke of Rosie as privileged, from a well-to-do background – that sort of thing, which was not really relevant. It was completely overlooked that her father was a hard-working professional man. This was something the judge fell for.
LL:	Would you agree, Rosie, that you were breaking the law and ought to be punished?
RJ:	There is no doubt that anybody who has anything to do with drugs knows that they are breaking the law.
LL:	How far do you believe that people in your circle at that time did not think of breaking the law relating to drugs in the same way as if they had been stealing, for example?
RJ:	When you steal, you are taking something from seombody else. But when you take drugs, you are doing harm to yourself.
LL:	To put it briefly: You were given nine months' imprisonment for acting as a messenger for your best friend – as an act of friendship. Your friend died of drink and an accidental overdose of drugs. The case aroused an enormous amount of interest in the press. But tremendous goodwill was generated, so in a sense life for you in prison was made more bearable?

RJ: As in any sort of microcosmic world, great generosity of spirit was often shown to me. But it was not just me.

LL: On the other hand, there is the negative side of celebrity. Were some people just jealous of you?

RJ: There were some people like that.

LL: You obviously provided some excitement in the prison.

RJ: On the whole, it is better to be a celebrity than not – to be the right kind of celebrity, that is. A lot of the cases you read about in the press, cases of child abuse, cruelty to children – if the woman is sentenced for child abuse and sent to Holloway, she is put under Rule 43 [solitary confinement] for her own safety.

LL: You had a very loving and supportive family, but was that too a source of pain because of your sensitivity to the fact of your mother's suffering?

RJ: In that situation, it is easier for the person going through the ordeal than for those who imagine what it is like. You yourself know what the actual situation is.

LL: Then you were feeling for your mother. But it is better to have a strong, supportive family. We then come to the factor of your being upper class – a cultured person. In your book you describe your companions in prison: did you have a worse time because they were so alien?

RJ: When I went into prison, I was expecting the very worst that could be imagined. So everything that happened was a kind of plus. Although they were alien, they were a good deal better than I had expected.

LL: But you did suffer a lot?

RJ: In proportion, the girls who were unpleasant were fewer than those who were nice.

LL: At any rate, you did feel as you write in your book that it was an awful experience. Do you think that it would be so for anyone else?

SJ: It is more of a stain for women going into prison.

LL: You don't feel a stain in having gone to prison?

RJ: I have written a book and turned the experience to my advantage.

LL: I suppose that you have a great feeling of injustice still?

RJ: I have to be very careful. If I allowed myself to dwell on that, I would become very bitter.

SJ: I don't believe you should allow yourself to think too much about injustice. I feel more deeply about the method of sentencing. I think it was cruel. I had never before seen such an example of cruelty. It is all done to humiliate the defendant.

RJ: It is very difficult to draw the line – to decide whether the judge was trying to humiliate me or to boost himself.

LL: Now we come to prison conditions. What struck me was how nasty the 'screws' were. They come out rather badly in your book.

RJ: I tried to be very balanced about that. I did try to come to some conclusions: what made people become prison officers? It is a very peculiar kind of person who wants to do that job. In the three prisons in which I was, the more punitive and pernicious 'screws' were in the open prison [East Sutton Park]. They were diabolical.

LL: Do you think conditions in open prisons are worse?

RJ: What puzzles me most is that men in an open prison have a much easier time of it – they come and go as they please.

LL: Were you not allowed to wander around?

RJ: You can escape if you really want to. People run away all the time.

SJ: Did it make it harder for you, knowing that you could walk out?

RJ: You can get out, but it means having a month tacked on to your sentence. If you walk out, you are known as being 'on your toes'. The majority of the women who do actually abscond go to see their children and the police know how to find them.

LL: Going back to the 'screws' . . .

RJ: They do behave appallingly and I do agree that having more responsibility is valid. I think, too, it was partly because at East Sutton they were younger – average age twenty-three. At Bullwood Hall they were a little older.

LL: If you were Home Secretary or were called on by the Home Secretary to advise him as to what should be done to improve matters, what would you do?

RJ: I would certainly suggest having more probation officers, instead of sending people to prison.

LL: But once they are in prison, do you see any way to improve things?

RJ: A lot could be done to produce a better attitude on the part of the staff. Prison officers complain that all the more agreeable work is being taken over by auxiliaries.

LL: Did you find that people like chaplains or doctors were more enlightened than the 'screws'?

RJ: Prison officers, because of their notion of their role, find it more difficult to communicate. The chaplains were brilliant. They had a much easier task of it because they had a unique role in the prison system – they knew what they were trying to do.

LL: Open prisons are supposed to be more enlightened, but from your account they sound like a most unenlightened regime. How far is that the fault of the Governor?

RJ: He/she may have the final decision over a central prison policy, but when it comes down to detail, the Governor really does not have very much control at all. No personal contact.

LL: What could be done? Would more education . . . ?

RJ: Definitely more education. There should be a complete revision of what the role of prisons is. Everything is so segregated and chopped up.

LL: People used to think that prisons could be used to reform people, but are now rather cynical about that.

RJ: If you accept that prisons are going to continue, then there should be considerably more reform within the prisons themselves, more preparation for release – much more gradual preparation, more education, more facilities altogether. Time spent in prison is not spent at all constructively.

LL: Take your fellow prisoners – were they thinking of going back?

RJ: Yes. A very great many said: 'See you again later!'

LL: What could you have done for them?

RJ: Well, there were courses in cookery, typing and so on, but they often did not take place. This side of life needs to be developed. There should be much more consideration given to trying to develop skills.

LL: The people among whom you found yourself were pretty hard nuts – people who won't often respond. What about afterwards? When you came out you had a strong supportive family and possibilities. Do you think more could be done to help these people when they come out?

RJ: Quite a lot is being done by people like APEX, NACRO, the New Bridge. It all comes down to money in the end. NACRO is underfunded and understaffed. A lot is left to the prisoner as to whether he wants to become involved with these groups. But many people lack motivation; there is also very little information available about these things. It is easier to re-offend if you do not have the information and nowhere to go to get support.

LL: The fact that there is just one man responsible for prisons – the Home Secretary – means that he has not got much time to give to them; there are too many other demands on him. Prisons need the full attention of one minister.

     Coming back to the stigma question. Do you think there is a stigma attaching to going to prison? Is this one of the more hurtful aspects?

RJ: Husbands were particularly concerned about this when their wives were involved. Women always think the judge is prejudiced against them – the usual male attitude towards women, the tension between the sexes.

LL: I think women do suffer more and someone has got to stick up for them. Biological factors alone make life much more difficult for them. They generate more suffering.

SJ: Coming back to the offender – the caring professions are incredibly poorly paid. Many people leave because they cannot survive on their pay. This should really be a government priority.

LL: The government are trying to reorganize the Probation Service, which is much resented by the probation officers.

SJ: I am a support worker for the Probation Service in Swindon.

LL: Was Rosie's experience what inspired you to do this work?

SJ: Yes. I felt the gross injustice of hearing of more and more cases of inadequate people committing crimes who should never have been sent to prison.

RJ: It is only when you become involved with prison that you realise the injustice of so many cases.

SJ: Rosie's friends were all appalled and supportive, but some of our friends ditched us. People in their fifties seem obsessed with success – they are 'on' to success and because we fought very hard to save Rosie from going to prison, there was quite definitely a feeling that we were failures of a certain kind with a very, very small number of people. We did find out who our true friends were. You very seldom demand the loyalty of your friends in life. I think the few who fell by the wayside were people who, on the whole, had very little confidence in themselves and were scared of associating with an underdog.

You had this extraordinary thing of the generations breaking down. People in their eighties were understanding and supportive and I made a great number of friends of a much higher calibre. I do definitely remember being much more dependent on my family and being conscious of the importance of the family, which made me feel incredibly privileged. Brothers and sisters are there in a crisis.

LL: I had forgotten how much press interest there was. It is difficult to believe that everyone flocked to your support. And it all arose from the tragedy of the death of a friend.

SJ: Socially I found it terribly interesting and again, it seemed to us a great sadness to have lost a few friends. But now we have benefited. We know a new sort of person we had not had very much to do with before all this.

LL: But not many of your generation dropped you, Rosie?

RJ: No, they were much more tolerant.

SJ: I think people of my age were shocked that we had a child in prison – the prison stigma. Yet if Rosie had only been put on probation, they would have said that she had got off.

    I have come to the conclusion that all punishment is evil. Penalties are fair enough, but I don't think that punishment should be any affair of the State. Too much blame is being dished around all over the place.

LL: People who do terrible things can't just be called 'mental'. If you take a gang rape, if you take that sort of thing, they have got to be punished.

RJ: To make sure they don't do it again.

SJ: In the Probation Service every single one of the good results we get has had nothing to do with punishment. Encouragement, interest, education, caring for them and loving them has produced the results I have seen.

LL: I call it punishment – but it is a matter of words really. I agree with the idea of punishment in the community, but the Probation Service hate that word 'punishment'. A Home Office official said that when the proposal for punishment in the community was first drafted it was called 'supervision in the community'. The ministers called it 'punishment in the community', as this was the only way to get the judges to agree.

SJ: Judges are on the whole maimed characters.

RJ: Prison officers similarly.

SJ: It is terribly sad that being a judge should be synonymous with getting a knighthood.

LL: Do you feel that Lord Lane [the Lord Chief Justice] is maimed?

SJ: No. He conducted the appeal decently, but did not allow it. I know there has to be a legal system, but if only they would stop calling it justice. The symbol of the scales and weights – there is nothing there to do with justice at all. The scales over the Old Bailey ought to come down. I find it a disgrace to see Her Majesty's coat of arms on all those appalling buildings without lavatories.

It is impossible to find a typical prisoner, just as it would be impossible to find a typical member of the House of Lords. Throughout her short time in prison, Rosie was a celebrity. Most prisoners, unless they are well-known villains, suffer from anonymity and obscurity. She was, as by now will be evident, sustained by a very loving family. On the other hand, she suffered through their sufferings. Neither she nor any other prisoner could ever say the last word about prisons. But her sensitivity, recollection of dialogue and gift of writing make her experience of real value to anyone anxious to improve our prison system.

Kim Wan

Kim Wan, today a successful businessman, at one time a cat burglar, has had an extraordinary career which surely equips him to say valuable things about punishment and the punished. Born in Singapore, he was educated for a time in a Chinese monastery. Coming to England, he became a fighter pilot in the war and was twice decorated. But he describes himself as being always a rebel, doing things in his own way. When he was demobilized, he came to the West End and 'lived it up on the strength of my gratuities – very much a womanizer'.

His money ran out, he fell into dubious company and was introduced to his first venture – breaking into cars. But this was no good. 'I wanted to get my hands on real money.' He became desperate and started to get involved with the underworld. 'Street girls offered to keep me, but my pride forbade that.' For three or four years he lived on crime. He became known as 'the No. 1 climber or creeper' – in other words, cat burglar. He then progressed to safe-cracking using explosives. To cut the story short, after serving more than one prison sentence and having escaped more than once, he was sentenced to seven years in Dartmoor. A violent prisoner, he was kept in a strait-jacket there for seven days at a time.

I began by asking Kim Wan when he had decided to renounce crime. His answer must be given in his own words: 'Very important this. You have to believe what I am going to say absolutely. I was in a punishment wing, in a strait-jacket – a very painful experience. You can't move at all. Lying on my back, at about one o'clock in the morning, wide awake, with the gaslights going up and down, an incredible thing came through – I have had this happen to me three times. I was thinking about my life, very fed up, thinking about my "bird" [sentence], when on the ceiling above me I saw a painting that could have been by Raphael or da Vinci. I thought I had created something new. I had a clear picture of something I had never seen before. At first it was not so clear, then it came to resemble the picture *The Virgin of the Rocks*. The painting seemed to be coming towards me, saying: Just have faith. That was my religious conversion. Afterwards I painted the vision myself.' May I add that Kim's painting is quite beautiful.

I am rather surprised that he has not pursued that vocation further. I asked him whether from that moment he decided to turn over a new leaf. His reply amounted to saying 'yes'. 'When I came out of the Air Force I was an arrogant, boastful, selfish man, but not a nasty man. I have worked it all out now. That vision was a mystical experience.'

When he eventually left prison, Kim devoted himself to rescuing ex-prisoners from their way of life. One anecdote must be recounted to illustrate his sincerity. He was invited to attend a meeting at the headquarters of the old Prison Commission. One of the officials present said to him: 'There are a number of ex-prisoners who come from long-term prisons, but we then lose touch with them.' Kim drew the conclusion, rightly or wrongly, that he was being asked to spy on his former colleagues. 'I kicked the chair over and said, "Naff, naff, I'm straight!"' He walked out. The official followed and apologized. He was then invited to discuss how ex-prisoners could best be assisted.

Now came the inevitable question from me. We were talking of punishment. 'Do you accept the view that prison never does anybody any good?' Kim's first reply was emphatic: 'Not the least bit of good!' He went on to say, however, that the violent men should be sorted out from the others. He recognized the acuteness of the problem. 'Most violent men, if you give them the maximum sentence – it will not convert them, but only make them ten times worse. If you are kind to them, they think you are a fool.' Naturally I pressed him as to what he would do. His reply took this form: 'Half their sentence should be done on productive work and the remaining half under some form of reformative teaching. They have to have enlightenment.' He recognizes to the full that in most cases they have had a very unsatisfactory home background. The father has usually been to blame. But from his own experience he has found that you can help them to make their way to a new kind of life.

Kim Wan is such an individual personality that it is best to draw from him and his methods a general lesson. More than once in our meeting he came back to an insistence on the soul. If you recognize the soul in a fellow human being, you are well on your way to bringing about his redemption from crime. He would agree that there are thousands of people in prison who should not be there and who would be far better doing service in the community. But whether in the community or in prison, if Kim Wan were in control, he would look for the soul in every man and in every woman.

John Masterson

John Masterson, a Scot, is a former violent prisoner who spent 187 days in an experimental Control Unit at Wakefield prison. The unit's harsh regime was designed to break even the most recalcitrant offender. After protests at the inhumanity of this from a great many penal agencies, the unit was closed down in 1975, fourteen months after it was opened.

John is now a reformed character concerned with the reform of others.

Lord Longford:	What would be your first reaction to the news of the Strangeways riots?
John Masterson:	I am surprised that it has not happened sooner. I have been in Strangeways – in 1974 I spent fourteen days in solitary confinement there, before being sent to the Control Unit at Wakefield.
LL:	Why were you in the solitary block?
JM:	I was never charged with breaking any prison rules. I had a dispute with the No. 1 Governor after the riots at Hull – there were three prisoners on the roof at Hull. I went to see the Governor and said I felt that the Governor was responsible for the prisoners being on the roof. I said the rules had been forgotten. I was then transferred to Strangeways where I had regular visits from a doctor, Roman Catholic priest and the Governor. With hindsight they were trying to see if I was a candidate for the special Control Unit at Wakefield, then in the experimental stage. I became the first prisoner to go to the Control Unit. It was 1974.
LL:	How long were you there?
JM:	187 days.

LL: Can you say a word about the unit? What was the idea behind it?

JM: The idea was to break men mentally and physically – psychological warfare.

LL: How different was it from the ordinary solitary unit under Rule 43?

JM: You were not allowed to speak. It took me a week to find out that there were two other prisoners in the unit.

LL: Were you not supposed to speak to anyone – not even staff?

JM: No. But two days before Dr Edith Summerskill, then Minister for Prisons, was due to pay a visit of inspection, they stopped this. You could not see out of the cell windows and the cell was all one colour.

LL: Were you locked up in there twenty-four hours a day?

JM: No, for twenty-three hours for the first ninety days. There was one hour for exercise.

LL: This was all eventually abandoned as being too inhuman. In the case of Strangeways, the riots are said to be due to overcrowding. Do you think there is anything else about the regime there apart from overcrowding which may be particularly bad?

JM: The attitude of staff and their unpleasant manner towards prisoners creates instability.

LL: This unpleasant attitude on the part of the staff – is this the general rule, or is it aggravated by over-crowding?

JM: Overcrowding makes prison life intolerable from a humanitarian point of view – degrading. But there is one compensation – in one way it tends to benefit prisoners because it makes it difficult for prison officers to single out individual prisoners, to victimize anyone.

LL: How old were you when you went into an institution?

JM: I was nineteen when I first went to Borstal.

LL: Had you been in trouble with the law before then?

JM: Only for minor charges.

LL: Looking back, why do you think that you found yourself in Borstal?

JM: I was always a rebel. My family background was strict, my parents both very religious. I was high-spirited, full of fun, loved playing practical jokes. I was a ringleader and always seemed to take the blame. The best part of my life was when I worked four years in the coal mines at fifteen until I was nineteen. Then I robbed a pub – pinched the takings.

LL: Do you feel, looking back, that this could have been avoided if you had been properly handled? Do you think it was because of maltreatment by society?

JM: My family had a lot to do with it. I had a religious upbringing, strict chapel. They had always been law-abiding. I got into trouble and they would not forgive me. It had an effect on me as a youngster – I was the naughty one.

LL: So the fact that they were so strict made you all the more rebellious because they could not understand you? When you came out of Borstal what did you do?

JM: I went back to the coal mines, but because of my disgrace it was difficult for me to settle down at home. I left home, and came to England, to Birmingham.

LL: How did you get on then?

JM: I got 'time' in Birmingham, a couple of prison sentences – four years was for a wages snatch. During my time in Birmingham prison, I had been twice on the roof and smashed up two cells.

LL: You were considered a violent man?

JM: I had seen a Home Office circular instruction stating that prisoners could have as much bread as they could eat. Until then the official ration had been five slices. When I got to the hotplate, the prisoner dishing out the bread only gave me five slices and I said I wanted ten. I took another five myself. The prison officer supervising ordered me to put them back. I explained about the Home Office instruction. I was totally in the right, but the prison officer did not agree. So I seized the bread, the hotplate and all that was on it and flung the lot over him. After that I was put in a strait-jacket. I became thoroughly bloody-minded over that injustice.

LL: What happened after that?

JM: I was transferred to other prisons – I have been in nineteen prisons altogether.

LL: Would you describe yourself as a violent prisoner?

JM: No, as a professional prisoner. I was never a professional criminal. I reacted hot-headedly to unfair treatment.

LL: After a number of years in nineteen prisons you found yourself in a Control Unit. Did you go to other prisons after that?

JM: They tried to keep me in Wakefield, but I only lasted four days in the ordinary section. On 23 December 1983, after you gave me lunch, I made the conscious decision never to go back to prison.

LL: Did you decide not to go back before or after lunch?

JM: After the lunch I felt like going back!

LL: From that day onwards how did you see things? We are taking you as someone who has been punished in all these ways and decided to renounce crime. From 1983 to 1990, how has it gone? You have had only one minor lapse which did not result in a prison sentence.

JM: Yes. Dispute over a bus fare.

LL: Looking back, what do you think produced this decision? If we could find the answer we could help other prisoners. Was your decision not to go back connected with a policy – or what?

JM: I think my age played a part in it. I was forty-one. In my last sentence I did not find other prisoners loyal. It is difficult to explain. The fact of the matter is, I had had enough of prison life and prisoners.

LL: Perhaps your early training in religion was coming out? You had had an early training in morality to start with.

JM: I was so involved with the prison system over the years – suffered under Rule 43 . . .

LL: If you were Home Secretary, how would you tackle the prison problem?

JM: I would tackle it in this sense: I would categorize certain crimes, so that certain prisons would be set apart for certain crimes – sex offenders should be in one special prison. I've clubbed a sex offender before now. The feeling that prisoners get is that you are mixed up with people the law considers to be monsters in society – those who interfere with children. Other prisoners who have only perhaps robbed out of sheer necessity resent this.

LL: You would not club them now?

JM: I wouldn't do it now.

LL: Take the people in Strangeways. Can you understand why they maltreated the sex offenders? Can you understand that?

JM: I can understand it, because when you are in prison for burglary or robbery of some kind which you have done to survive, society sends sex offenders to the same prison and you are all classed the same. Prisoners feel that crimes against humanity are different from those in the criminal system – prisoners feel revulsion against sex offenders. They feel they are being classed with them and society identifies them together. There should be certain prisons for certain crimes.

This is one common point between prisoners and the staff. Prison staff will tip off prisoners: 'So-and-so is a sex case.' Some sex cases receive press publicity, but some do not and they last as long as it takes for the rest to learn that they are sex offenders.

LL: Is there a way of treating people like yourself which would have led you to abandon crime much earlier? Is there a way of approaching people like you to give up crime?

JM: I consider that the basics of life – family, a roof over your head and work – are a must. Most people who come to prison have no ties in the outside world – no roof, no work. If you have no roof over your head, you can't get work. It is difficult to live a decent life if you have no ties – something you would lose if you went to prison. If you have no sense of loss except your freedom you are a dangerous prisoner.

LL: You imply that people take to crime because they cannot get on in the outside world – but what about those who do so out of greed? Coming back to yourself, young men, young rebels like you – if people had tried to help you, would you have responded?

JM: The punitive attitude of society towards those who have committed crimes reflects itself in the attitude of the prison staff.

LL: I do see a difference between the attitude of staff in a prison and in a special hospital.

JM: The attitude of the staff produces on the part of the prisoner a feeling of injustice. He comes to believe that he is not so much the wrongdoer as the victim. The attitude of the staff justifies his attitude to society; he ends up with no respect for anyone, because he has not been treated with respect. He has no feeling of guilt; he has been overpunished.

IV

Punishment and the Punished

I Provisional Reflections

The men and women who have given evidence to me are, with one important exception, agreed on one proposition, namely that sentencing policy in Britain is too severe and that too many of our penal troubles flow from that. It is frequently said that we have far too many people in prison, but that is another way of saying that the judiciary send far too many people there. Once when I said something to this effect in the House of Lords, Lord Hailsham retorted that the prisoners who committed the crimes were the main culprits. That is true, of course, but given the existing amount of crime, almost everyone with any claims to being a penal reformer is agreed that our judiciary, compared with other European countries, punish offenders too severely.

Taking the witnesses as a whole, there is a general disposition to criticize – castigate is not too strong a word – our present prison system. But with two important exceptions, the general attitude is almost equally critical. The important exceptions are Lord Windlesham, former Home Office minister and former Chairman of the Parole Board, and Mr Alan Eastwood, Chairman of the Police Federation. Their views should be studied with very close attention, although in certain respects they are different from mine. Peter Thompson and Edward Fitzgerald have discussed the problem of mental offenders with specialist knowledge.

If I had to single out an issue on which well-informed persons are likely to differ in the penal area, it is the question of whether the 'rehabilitative ideal' has now been discredited. Whatever the language used, the idea that prison can function as a reforming agency would seem to be equally rejected by the ex-prisoners questioned and by witnesses such as Lord Windlesham and Mary Tuck of the Home Office Research and Planning Unit. But an answer is swiftly given by those who have had or who continue to have the closest administrative connection with prisons.

Peter Timms, for example, former Governor of Maidstone, and David Evans, General Secretary of the Prison Officers' Association, say emphatically that reform in prison has not failed, just as Christianity has not failed – *it has never been tried*. The ideal of Judge Tumim, Chief Inspector of Prisons, under which all punishment in prisons should be a form of training, is far from achievement in the near future. Peter Thompson, Director of the Matthew Trust, goes further than anyone else, and further than I do, in saying that all prisoners are sick people.

I am myself more and more convinced that prison as a form of treatment will always be much less constructive than the best kind of treatment outside. But however far one looks into the future, we are going to have many thousands of men and women in prison. The movement towards punishment in the community must on no account be allowed to obscure the splendid work that has been done in prisons and the much more splendid work that could be done in the future.

Punishment in the community, however, raises the question of who is to conduct the supervision required. There can only be one answer to that question – the Probation Service. But the utmost sensitivity and tact will need to be employed if probation officers are to be persuaded to cooperate in a task which, at first sight, seems to many of them to be opposed to their traditions.

But now let us turn to some of the key issues in the administration of justice.

II *Sentencing*

Again and again in this book I keep returning to sentencing. Until recently it did not figure much in penal discussion, but now it occupies the centre of the stage. Practically every discussion on how to reduce the prison population concludes that the judiciary must be induced to be much less severe in their sentencing policy.

It would be disingenuous not to recognize in the Britain of the 1990s another widely held view, based on untutored gut reaction. On Friday 6 July 1990, following England's defeat in the semi-finals of the World Cup, the *Sun* declared GIVE THUGS FIVE YEARS. It went on:

> How can it happen? How can natural disappointment over a lost soccer game spill over into a rampage of violence and destruction in a score of our cities? Two English players miss penalty kicks far away in Turin and a man is MURDERED in Southampton. A pub landlady in Brighton is so appalled by the wrecking of a rampaging mob that she suffers a HEART ATTACK and dies. Why, why, why?

The *Sun*'s conclusion is stark:

> The law provides tough sentences for violent crime. However, we have a strange new breed of judges whose concern for the criminal is greater than their concern to protect the victims. . . . Parliament and the Government should lay down minimum sentences beyond the discretion of weak courts.

That is an argument I regard with horror. All research, official and otherwise in recent years, has demonstrated, in so far as such a proposition can ever be demonstrated, that long sentences do not increase the deterrent effect of punishment.

A most thorough discussion of sentencing policy is provided in *Sentencing – A Way Ahead*, a report by the lawyers' society, Justice. The chairman of the committee was Lady Ralphs, Vice-Chairman of the Magistrates' Association. A retired High Court judge was included in a powerful team of magistrates, academics and practising lawyers.

Their attitude to the present position can be illustrated in these three sentences:

> If judicial discretion in sentencing is not to be totally unfettered, it must be exercised within the context of a coherent rationale arising from some underlying philosophy. The May Committee failed to find one, and Parliament has shown marked reluctance to provide one. . . . Unfortunately the sentencing system built on the foundation of rehabilitation and containing the wide judicial discretion regarded as necessary to pursue this objective has not been reformed to reflect the reality relating to the pursuit of this objective.

The committee enunciated six fairly orthodox objectives of sentencing:

1. Retribution
2. Denunciation
3. Deterrence
4. Protection (of society)
5. Rehabilitation
6. Reparation

They made thirty-three recommendations, of which I will single out four. The first two address the question of how to reduce the numbers in prison.

1. The premise that prison is a punishment of last resort should be firmly established and acted upon. Courts should send to prison only those whose offences are so grave that any lesser

sentence would be unacceptable. This proposal would presumably apply to adults the same kind of legislation that has been so successful in the last five years in reducing the number of juveniles and young offenders in custody.

2. Maximum penalties should be revised so that the gravest offences carry the more severe penalties. The more severe penalties should relate to violent or sexual offences rather than to property offences which involve no threat to the person. One must hope that under this proposal there would be a general reduction in the average level of maximum sentences.

3. Widespread support is growing for the third recommendation: 'A Sentencing Commission should be created with the task of drawing up guidelines and monitoring, evaluating and updating them.' In principle, this is an excellent suggestion. It is not clear, however, how far guidelines laid down by a Sentencing Commission would be binding on the courts. To what extent could a prisoner get his sentence set aside if it were held (on appeal?) that the sentence was in conflict with the guidelines of the Commission? The committee make a strenuous effort to harmonize the sentencing attitudes to be expected from the judiciary and Parliament. How precisely all that would work out is again not obvious.

4. There is a more serious difficulty with another recommendation to which the committee obviously attach high importance: 'The rationale underlying all the principles of sentencing should be that of proportionality.' Punishment should be proportionate to the gravity of the offence and the culpability of the offender. Does this mean, however, that of the six objectives of sentencing given above, the first one, retribution, should be dominant over the others? If so, this is unacceptable. There is a place for retribution, but certainly not a role which makes it supreme.

At this point, let us turn to a debate on sentencing levels which I initiated in the House of Lords on 23 May 1990. In my speech I

emphasized the familiar points and submitted the familiar conclusion: somehow or other, the judiciary must be induced to send
fewer people to prison and for shorter periods. I called attention to
three (among other) ways of bringing this about, so that it would
be much more difficult for judges to send people to prison without
giving very good reasons.

First, we could reduce maximum sentences.

Secondly, we could pass legislation similar to that which has
been so effective in reducing the number of young adults and
juveniles in custody. And thirdly, we could establish some kind of
Sentencing Council. There is no room for dogmatism about the
form this should take. Let me interpolate here a passage from a
memorandum published by NACRO called *Criteria for Custody*
(April 1990):

> A number of factors have contributed to the fall in the number
> of custodial sentences imposed on young offenders since 1983.
> These include a reduction in the number of juveniles in the
> general population; a fall in the juvenile crime rate; the de-
> velopment of intensive intermediate treatment schemes for
> juveniles; the establishment of inter-agency committees, in-
> cluding representatives of the magistracy, justices' clerks, the
> probation service, social services and voluntary organisations
> to plan the development of these schemes; the development of
> probation day centres for offenders aged seventeen and over;
> the extension of community service orders to sixteen-year-olds;
> and systematic work by the probation service and social ser-
> vices departments to target intensive non-custodial measures
> on offenders genuinely at risk of custody, and to improve the
> quality and clarity of social inquiry reports recommending such
> measures to the courts.

According to NACRO, 'the government's White Paper, *Crime,
Justice and Protecting the Public* [February 1990], proposes to extend
similar statutory criteria to the sentencing of adult offenders.' If
this proves to be the case under new legislation, the beneficial
results should be far-reaching.

To return to our debate in the House of Lords: We were

fortunate in securing the participation of the Law Lord, Lord Ackner, one of the sharpest minds in the House. I had made the draft of my speech accessible to the Law Lords. Lord Ackner bravely responded by informing us that 'so courteous and elegant a gauntlet could hardly be ignored'. His speech must be held to provide a summary of the judiciary's current attitude to sentencing. It was too much to expect that they would crudely admit that their sentencing had hitherto been too severe and they would now turn over a new leaf.

Lord Ackner made light of the comparisons with other countries which are so often used to support the claim that we send too many people to prison in this country. In so far as he accepted comparisons at all, he argued with strong conviction that 'the sentences given in other countries . . . would have been strongly criticized if given in England'. In other words, the present sentencing levels are in accord with public opinion.

When Viscount Ullswater, the Home Office minister, came to reply for the government he was faced with two questions: 1) Did the government agree that the time had come for a new approach to sentencing? 2) Were the government ready to repudiate the heavy increase in the prison population forecast by the Home Office after the White Paper *Crime, Justice and Protecting the Public* was published? The minister's reply was diplomatic. In the light of Lord Justice Woolf's current investigation, one could hardly expect it to be very forthcoming. He insisted that 'the White Paper does not reflect an underlying lack of confidence in the way the courts sentence offenders'. He admitted that there was, on the face of it, considerable discrepancy between the sentences handed out by different courts. He claimed, however, that this was diminishing. 'There is already considerable consistency of approach in sentencing by Crown Court judges. It is on this that we wish to build.'

As regards the question of whether a *new* approach to sentencing was desirable, Viscount Ullswater continued in his diplomacy: 'The White Paper proposals are indeed very significant but they do not represent a radically new approach. They build on developments which have taken place over the last ten years. The Court of Appeal has encouraged a more consistent approach to sentencing in its recent guideline judgements on rape, drug trafficking and incest. The structured approach to sentencing decisions which the Court of Appeal has used has been a helpful development which has influenced our thinking.'

Let us not labour the semantic issue: doctrines never change; they *develop*. Far more important, however, is whether the government are setting out to secure a major reduction in the prison population in practice. When challenged with the disquieting Home Office forecast in spring 1990 after the publication of *Crime, Justice and the Protection of the Public*, which predicted that the prison population would rise by 12,000 by 1997–8, the minister confirmed the forecast but left us completely uncertain whether the government still accepted it. Since then, the Home Office has published a revised forecast of an increase of 7500 by 1998.

The one definite thing the minister said, and this was most regrettable, was his rejection of a Sentencing Council. The government 'see no need for such a body'. One can only hope that after the Woolf Report the present government, if still in power, will see these matters in a new light.

But let us regard the whole speech as a holding operation and one intended at all costs to carry along the judiciary. 'The courts,' Viscount Ullswater said, 'will need to retain a wide discretion if they are to continue to deal justly with the great variety of crimes that come before them. For that reason, we reject a rigid, statutory framework of mandatory or of minimal sentences.' Let us hope that this is in no way the government's last word on the subject.

If the government mean business when they talk of reducing the population in prison, they will at least announce a target, though no one supposes that targets can always be achieved. If asked to name a figure, I would suggest the opposite of the Home Office's spring calculations. In other words, not an increase but a reduction in the number of prisoners in the next six or seven years. And, of course, I would hope to see much greater reductions in the years beyond.

Unless or until that happens, or some other target is announced, I shall remain sceptical of the government's approach, hoping however that I will be proved wrong.

III   Five Crucial Issues

PAROLE

No one who writes about criminal justice can ignore parole. The *locus classicus* of the parole system will always be *The Parole System in England and Wales*, a Report of the Review Committee under the Chairmanship of Lord Carlisle of Bucklow.

Lord Carlisle referred to parole as 'selective early release on licence' and referred to *The Adult Offender*, the 1965 White Paper which outlined the government's proposals at the time. They eventually became law in the Criminal Justice Act of 1967.

> The 1965 White Paper proposed that 'a prisoner who has shown promise or determination to reform . . . should be able to earn a further period of freedom on parole [i.e., over and above the one-third remission] of up to one-third of his sentence'. The merits of the new scheme were expressed in rehabilitative terms: 'prisoners who do not have of necessity to be detained for the protection of the public are in some cases more likely to be made into decent citizens if, before completing the whole of their sentence, they are released under supervision with a liability to recall if they do not behave . . . What is proposed is that a prisoner's date of release should be largely dependent on his response to training and his likely behaviour on release.'

The Carlisle Report, which was presented to Parliament by the Home Secretary in November 1988, makes a number of proposals which would give effect to suggestions made by penal reformers over the years. Above all, it recommends that reasons should be given when parole is refused; at present, the Parole Board's findings are confidential and the applicant has no right to be informed of them.

The outstanding result, however, of the Carlisle Committee's recommendations would be to bring about a cataclysmic reduction in the number of applicants for parole, because in future only certain categories of offender would be eligible to apply for it. Applications would come down from 24,000 a year to 4000. In the words of the report:

All those sentenced to 4 years or less should serve a fixed proportion of their sentence in custody, subject to release being delayed for specific misbehaviour in prison. Parole should be available only to those sentenced to more than 4 years. . . . For those sentenced to more than 4 years the parole eligibility date should be at one-half of sentence rather than one-third as it is now. . . . All offenders sentenced to 4 years' imprisonment or less should be required to serve half the sentence in custody, plus any additional days for specific misconduct in prison, and half in the community.

I agree that parole does not make sense in the case of very short sentences, where improvement on the part of the prisoner can hardly be identified. But the reduction called for by Carlisle would take the heart out of the whole parole system. One questions whether parole would long survive in any form. In short, this basic recommendation is disastrous.

I may be biased, subconsciously perhaps, in my reaction. Parole was introduced in the 1967 Criminal Justice Act as part of a package of measures which had the common theme of 'keeping out of prison those who need not be there' (Roy Jenkins, the Home Secretary, introduced the second reading). The Carlisle Report was kind enough to say: 'It was the 1964 report of a Labour Party Study Group under the chairmanship of Lord Longford, entitled *Crime – A Challenge to us All*, which seems to have made the first explicit call for the setting up of a fully-fledged system.' Six members of our committee became members, in due course, of the subsequent Wilson government, including the Lord Chancellor and Attorney-General.

I have myself always attached most importance to the potential moral influence of a parole system. The Carlisle Committee put that consideration in their own way: 'A possibility of parole provides a valuable means of motivating prisoners during their sentence and giving them a light at the end of the tunnel.' A further and strong argument for parole is that it can be relied upon to reduce the prison population. I have always been, therefore, and remain a strong believer in the principle of the parole system.

Over the years, particularly in America and recently in Britain also, many people have argued against the retention of the parole system. When the Carlisle Report was adopted in the House of Lords there was a good deal of support for its conclusions, in spite of the drastic reduction proposed. I was something of a lone voice in expressing disappointment and criticism. But in addition to the proposed reduction in the scope of parole, the committee were gravely handicapped by not being able to make recommendations about sentencing policy. They indicated that their proposals were formulated by the 'hope and expectation' – repeat: expectation – that sentences would be considerably reduced by the judiciary. If this does not occur, the proposals of the Carlisle Committee will be neutral in regard to the number of people retained in prison and might even increase that number, which one assumes the Carlisle Committee would regard most unhappily.

The report of the Carlisle Committee also makes another disastrous suggestion, namely that the local review committees, which assess a prisoner's suitability for parole, should be abolished. At the present time, one member of the committee meets the prisoner face to face. They are at least local people, including usually the Governor of the prison. The latter certainly knows a good deal about the prisoner. Under the Carlisle Report, the decision about the fate of the prisoner would be taken on the strength of documents alone, a lamentable idea.

For myself, I would:

1. Retain the local review committees.
2. Make arrangements for at least one member of the Parole

Board taking the final decision to meet any prisoner under discussion, if necessary by visiting him or her in prison.
3. Make arrangements for the prisoner to be assisted locally or otherwise in presenting his or her case. Like the Carlisle Committee, I would insist that reasons for a negative decision should be given.

I shall have more to say about parole in the next section dealing with murder and life imprisonment.

MURDER AND LIFE IMPRISONMENT

Prisoners serving a life sentence were excluded from the review of the Carlisle Committee on Parole. A Select Committee of the House of Lords, however, produced in October 1989 a report on murder and life imprisonment (the Nathan Report). Soon afterwards, it was debated in the House of Lords. In the long run its most important recommendation will be that life imprisonment should no longer be mandatory when a prisoner has been convicted of murder. With that, I entirely agree.

I accept, therefore, the view of the committee that in the vast majority of cases murderers should be given a determinate sentence, subject to parole. I accept also the corollary that life sentences should still be imposed in a limited number of cases. The committee, however, used language which is unacceptable or, at the very least, dangerous. I must quote their words:

The life sentence should remain available, both for particularly outrageous murders and for those where there would be a degree of uncertainty about the risk, by reason in particular of his mental condition, of releasing a prisoner at the end of a determinate sentence.

This view cannot be allowed to stand. We should at all times strongly resist any suggestion that human beings who are recognizably mentally afflicted should be sent to prison at all, let alone sent there for life. There is an implication, admittedly ambiguous, in the report that some prisoners at least who are not mentally afflicted should spend the rest of their lives in prison. That is in my eyes a detestable and most un-Christian idea.

Let me try to pull together what I wrote in the previous section about parole and what I am saying now about life imprisonment. No human justice is likely to be identified with Divine justice; it may not often approximate to it. But a properly organized judicial system provides the best answer, at the time of conviction, about the proper sentence which it seems at that moment the man or woman should serve.

This does not mean, however, that at some later date, perhaps a number of years later, the court's original opinion cannot be improved upon. Whether for life prisoners or others, a properly constituted parole system should be able to provide the best answer at the later date when far more is known about the prisoner than could possibly have been known at the time of conviction. What factors should be taken into account by the later tribunal? At the present time the factors being taken into account by the Parole Board are hidden from the public, except in the most general sense. As I have said, that should be put right in the future.

It is tempting to say that all a Parole Board should take into account is *risk*. In the words of Carlisle:

> The parole decision should be based on a more specific test than now, namely an evaluation of the risk to the public of the person committing further serious offences at a time when he would otherwise be in prison, against the benefit both to him and the public of his being released from prison back into the community under a degree of supervision which might assist his rehabilitation and thus lessen the risk of his re-offending in the future.

Certainly I do not think that it is a Parole Board's business to take into account such other elements in a just sentence as, for example, deterrence, prevention and retribution, but it is worth pausing for a moment over the meaning of *risk*. When the Labour Party Study Group which I chaired drew up the original proposals for parole in 1964, we were thinking mainly of providing a more humane treatment for prisoners and, above all, of encouraging them to lead more moral lives. Twenty-five years later the emphasis has passed in many minds to the protection of the public, which has a somewhat different implication.

Imagine two men, both convicted of the same offence and both making the same effort, with the same degree of success, to improve their conduct. Surely this means that they would have the same chance of parole. But if we are weighing up the risk in purely statistical terms, the one returning to a criminal home would represent a much greater risk of re-offending than one returning to an academic family in North Oxford. The dilemma, I am afraid, will persist. In solving it, some will lay their first emphasis on the supposed protection of the public. Others, including myself, will concentrate on human fairness.

There remains the question of the procedure for considering the release of prisoners serving life sentences. There is no obvious moment for their consideration, as there is in the case of prisoners serving a determinate sentence. As mentioned earlier (see page 14), Myra Hindley has twice been recommended for release on licence by the local review committee. The Parole Board have not only turned her down on both occasions but have also announced that she could not be considered for another five years. Bearing in mind the terrible crimes in which she was involved, and their savage exploitation by the media, Myra Hindley and others like her still have a claim to justice.

I myself consider that, after ten years, any prisoner should have the option of a public hearing before a judicial body with full legal aid available. No plan for providing justice for life prisoners is going to be free from objection, but the arrangements we have made for them until now are not those of a truly civilized society.

MENTAL OFFENDERS

Mental offenders have received less than their fair share of attention in these pages in spite of expert contributions from Peter Thompson and Edward Fitzgerald. Many penal problems are baffling, but that of mental offenders supremely so. They have been in my mind for many years; indeed since I first visited a lady, a family friend, in Broadmoor fifty years ago. In a fit of extreme depression, she had killed one of her children and tried to kill herself. She was judged unfit to plead and sent to Broadmoor. Later, she emerged and made a happy marriage. She would represent a fairly simple case. No one would suggest that she ought to have gone to prison or been left at large in the community.

Many years later, I supplied introductions to two books which Peter Thompson wrote after his time in Broadmoor. Much later again in 1988, I opened a debate in the House of Lords on mental offenders. I stated the problem then as I see it now: 'We punish those who break the law, we treat and try to heal those who are sick, but what of those who fall into both categories: they break the law, but are judged to be sick? How do we deal with them so as to protect society without imputing blame or full moral responsibility to them?'

Not long ago (July 1990), I was reading an article in *The Times* headed: *Suicides in Prison: Call for Reform for Mentally Ill*. It described a report produced by five leading pressure groups concerned with mental reform and the mentally ill. The report must be studied in detail, but broadly speaking it endorses the contentions of all penal reformers today (cf. Peter Thompson and Edward Fitzgerald above) that far too many men and women are in prison who ought to be receiving treatment in mental hospitals. That conclusion I accept unreservedly, as a result of my own prolonged experience of prisoners with mental troubles.

I accept just as unreservedly the need for much improved psychiatric facilities in prisons. We are left asking ourselves, however, who are to be regarded as mentally ill for this purpose? I have just been reading *Child Pornography*, an absorbing book by Tim Tate whose investigations had much to do with the 1987 change in the law which made the possession of child pornography illegal. He quotes poignantly from the evidence of a child molester, at that time incarcerated in a Californian prison, given to a US Senate Inquiry in February 1985: 'I hope no one thinks,' he told the Inquiry, 'that what I will say today is designed to win sympathy for myself. It isn't. Your sympathy should go to my victims – twenty-two little girls, ages six to fourteen, whom I've molested since 1949. They will likely carry the emotional scars for the rest of their lives.' Later, he went on to say: 'If I hadn't been under a psychiatrist's care part of the time, I probably would have committed suicide. The doctor helped me with my hate for my father and my fear of adult women, but he couldn't do anything about my desire for little girls.'

What label are we to apply to such a man – bad or mad, or very very sad? His own conclusion is depressing, but not quite hopeless: 'Like the alcoholic, there is no known cure for the paedophile. The paedophile must realize he has a problem and wants help.' A society with any claim to be Christian must give him and many like him far more help than they are receiving at present.

REMAND

Our penal system has been defended by few apart from official spokesmen in recent years. The remand system has been defended by none. It is now thirty years since Lord Stonham, sitting on the Opposition Front Bench in the House of Lords, referred to the 'hell-hole of Brixton', then as now the leading remand prison. Victor Stonham, a devoted friend of prisoners, became soon after this a Home Office minister. He had to adopt a slightly different tone, but I know well that he never changed his view about the iniquity of the remand position.

Many years later Lord Hutchinson, a former leader of the Criminal Bar, opened a debate in the Lords on the situation in Brixton. A number of us intending to speak made our way there and were horrified by what we found, although we were much impressed by the enlightened Governor and his attempts to make the best of a bad job. Soon afterwards, however, there were two sensational escapes from Brixton. Security, one presumes, was then seen as the most pressing objective. Things became worse than ever.

The story of the 1980s is a dismal one. A decade ago, in 1980, the average daily number of remand prisoners was 6438, which amounted to 15 per cent of the average prison population of 42,109. On 28 February 1990, 10,228 prisoners were awaiting trial or sentence in penal establishments in England and Wales. This constituted 22 per cent of the total prison population of 46,895. Of these prisoners, 8366 (8041 males and 325 females) were awaiting trial, while 1862 (1772 males and 90 females) were awaiting sentence. At the present time 40 per cent of all defendants, 39 per cent of male defendants and 54 per cent of female defendants remanded in custody do not subsequently receive a custodial sentence.

It would be wrong to suggest that no attempt has been made in recent years to improve matters. The Bail Act (1976) provides that a defendant should be granted bail unless he or she is likely to abscond, commit an offence on bail, interfere with witnesses or otherwise obstruct the course of justice. As a result of the Act, the annual number of remands in custody is lower than it was before the bail reforms of the mid 1970s. Despite this, however, the *average daily number* of remand prisoners is now much higher than it was a decade ago. This is because of the increasing length of time spent on remand. The average length of time spent in custody by an unconvicted male prisoner rose from thirty-six days in 1978 to fifty-six days in 1988. The equivalent figures for untried female prisoners were twenty-four days in 1978 and fifty-one days in 1988.

I have known many prisoners who have spent a year or more in custody awaiting trial. Of the two I have seen most of recently in Brixton, one spent more than a year there before going on trial. Another at the time of writing is awaiting trial after more than six months in custody.

It is dangerous to generalize, but in my experience remand prisoners do no work and spend something like twenty-one to twenty-two hours a day in their cells. No doubt a few such prisoners expect to be sentenced to imprisonment eventually and are happy to remain in custody for a long period, knowing that this will be counted against the length of their sentence. There are, admittedly, some advantages – daily visits are permitted, for example. The day before I wrote this, I visited Brixton. Behind me in the queue was a middle-aged, tired-looking woman. I asked her if she came to the prison often. 'Every day,' she said. 'But only for fifteen minutes.' Remand prisoners are allowed to wear their own clothes, although in my experience they frequently prefer not to. Nevertheless, the life of a prisoner on remand makes a total mockery of any claim that prison is a constructive agency.

I cannot imagine anyone – hard-hearted or soft-hearted – who does not agree that the present number of remand prisoners is a blatant scandal. Where does the blame lie? In one sense, as always in these matters, one has to go back to the facts of crime and its remorseless increase over the years. That being said, we can point a finger of accusation at judges and magistrates for refusing bail so often; at the politicians for not improving the law; and, above all, at those responsible for the appalling sluggishness of our legal system.

Again, one must not imply that no attempt has been made to improve matters. The Prosecution of Offences Act (1985) empowered the Home Secretary to introduce statutory time limits to criminal proceedings. They have in fact been introduced in a number of areas. The government intends to extend the time limits and the sooner it does so, the better. When a time limit expires, the defendant is entitled to bail unless a court extends the limit, which it can only do if it is satisfied that there is good and sufficient cause, and that the prosecution has acted with all due expedition.

There is general agreement that a great extension of the number of bail hostels would bring about a considerable reduction in the total of remand prisoners. So, I feel sure, would an extension of what are called bail information schemes. About these I will quote a Home Office circular, *Bail* (No. 25/1988), which states:

Often a remand in custody might be averted if the justices had more detailed information about, for example, the character of the defendant, or the conditions in which he would be living if he were released on bail. The early availability of relevant information could do much to satisfy the court that the general presumption in favour of bail should not be overruled, or that bail may properly be granted if relevant conditions are attached.

To sum up: the remand scandal must be tackled from a number of different angles, but until it is so tackled, the scandal remains. At the present time (December 1990) there is a suggestion that the government intends to move towards the privatization of the remand system. It is difficult to believe that there would be any economic advantages. Even if there were, it would be outrageous for anyone to make a profit out of punishing prisoners, and no one can deny that prisoners held on remand are being punished. I am happy to adopt the words used by the Prison Officers' Association: 'Private sector involvement in the remand system is ethically dubious and is likely to lead to the lowering of standards in both operational and security terms.'

CRIME, JUSTICE AND PROTECTING THE PUBLIC

Crime, Justice and Protecting the Public, the White Paper issued in February 1990, is the most serious attempt at a coherent penal policy produced in this country in my lifetime. In the last fifty years only two major reforms have improved the lot of convicted persons: the abolition of capital punishment in 1965 and the introduction of parole in 1968. According to the authorities I rely on most, the condition of prisoners today from the dreadful overcrowding is worse than it was thirty or thirty-five years ago. It would be worse still if there had not been considerable progress in the development of alternatives to custody.

The White Paper for the first time tries to tackle the penal question as a whole. It comes from a Conservative government, which leads me to diverge for a few moments and refer to the record of that Party in recent years. A Conservative Prime Minister, Sir Winston Churchill, was the boldest penal reformer among the Home Secretaries of this century, though admittedly he was a Liberal at the time (1909–11). Sir Samuel Hoare's period as Conservative Home Secretary was cut short by the

Second World War. Later he emerged as a very active President of the Howard League for Penal Reform.

R. A. Butler showed signs of being a great reforming Home Secretary when he took office in 1957, but he was distracted by a multitude of other responsibilities. William Whitelaw picked up the torch in 1979 and in particular showed signs of pressurizing the judges in the direction of lighter sentences. But to put it crudely, he 'got the bird' at the Conservative conference of 1981 which ended his role as a penal reformer.

His successor, Leon Brittan, went to the other extreme, having learned a painful lesson. His remodelling of the parole system and other steps have been denounced far and wide ever since. Douglas Hurd revealed enlightened inclinations. He stood up manfully at Party conferences against the loud demands for the return of capital punishment, which Mrs Thatcher made no secret of favouring. He and his Minister of State, John Patten, must be given credit for preparing the White Paper now before us. It is too early to say how the new Home Secretary, Kenneth Baker, will react to these far-reaching proposals, but he will be judged by his handling of them.

The problem before this government is to reduce substantially the number of prisoners without appearing to be 'soft' on crime. Any British government would be faced by the same sort of problem. But the sentiment associated with Conservative conferences makes the problem so much harder for a government of that complexion.

The present government seem to fear that public opinion will be opposed to any increasing 'softness', to any attempt, that is, to make life in prison more agreeable and to distance the sentencing policy of the judiciary from public sentiment. The solution in the Green Paper which preceded *Crime, Punishment and Protecting the Public* is a bold one. It is best described as 'punishment in the community'. In other words, the number of those serving sentences of imprisonment will be substantially reduced. But this does *not*, repeat *not*, mean that those released from custody will be spared punishment. On this plan, they will instead undergo their punishment in the community – an extension, it might be said, of the system of community service orders with which we are becoming familiar.

Differing from not a few penal reformers, I applaud the principle of punishment in the community, although I do not approve of particular devices – electronic 'tagging', for example. But the success of such a philosophy depends in the first place on the judiciary. They have got to be persuaded to make use of the new opportunities created. If they continue with present sentencing policies, the numbers in prison will not diminish and are likely to increase. In the second place, the Probation Service must be carried along as willing cooperators.

Lord Hunt of Llanfair Waterdine, who was President of the National Association of Probation Officers for many years, considers that the Probation Service has been handled heavy-handedly by the government in recent times (see pages 22–25). It would in theory be possible to create a new service committed whole-heartedly to punishment in the community. That way lies madness. It has to be recognized that 'punishment' as a description of part of their role repels large numbers of probation officers, perhaps the majority. Considerable diplomatic skill will be necessary if they are to be persuaded to throw themselves into the new forms of supervision required. It will not be easy, but it will be a tragedy if it is not achieved.

Punishment in the community is not the only new idea to be discovered in the government White Paper. Distinguishable from it is the new emphasis on 'just deserts', or 'retribution' as it has usually been called. At the time I wrote my book *The Idea of Punishment*, published thirty years ago, the concept of retribution was regarded as reactionary, even out of date, though I pleaded for it as an element in a just punishment, possibly under the name of fairness. It is now back with a vengeance, though vengeance is not a happy word in this connection (see the views of Lord Windlesham, page 20).

The relevant passages from *Crime, Justice and Protecting the Public* must be given at some length:

The government's aim is to ensure that convicted criminals in England and Wales are punished justly and suitably according to the seriousness of their offences; in other words, that they get their just deserts. No government should try to influence the courts in individual cases. The independence of the judiciary is rightly regarded as a cornerstone of our liberties. But sentencing principles and sentencing practice are matters of legitimate concern to government, and Parliament provides the funds necessary to give effect to the courts' decisions.

And the White Paper goes on to make its meaning still plainer:

Punishment in proportion to the seriousness of the crime has long been accepted as one of many objectives in sentencing. It should be the principal focus of sentencing decisions.

The White Paper seeks to link just deserts with punishment in the community. The government consider

that those who commit very serious crimes, particularly crimes of violence, should receive long custodial sentences; but that many other crimes can be punished in the community, with greater emphasis on bringing home to the criminal the consequences of his actions, compensation to the victim and reparation to the community.

But what, if any, is the connection between just deserts and punishment in the community rather than in custody? The clue lies in part of the evidence given to me by Mary Tuck, former Head of the Home Office Research and Planning Unit. Criminological research in recent years has been remarkably influential in a negative direction. It has discredited custody as an agency of reform and equally as an agency of deterrence. That does not mean that it has discredited punishment, though *how much* punishment should be administered (the *quantum* of punishment) is not something on which criminologists wish to pronounce.

There remains an argument for custody, which in America is called 'incapacitation' and which used to be known in Britain as 'prevention': the idea of keeping men and women in prison in order to render them unable to carry out further crimes. That could hardly be made the basis for a national penal policy, but there is a disquieting suggestion along these lines in the White Paper. Let me quote another passage:

> The government believes that there should be a sharper distinction between the severity with which the courts treat violent crime and property offences. . . . The government proposes to take this approach further by giving the Crown Court power to give custodial sentences longer than would be justified by the seriousness of the offence to persistent violent and sexual offenders, if this is necessary to protect the public from serious harm.

With this idea I profoundly disagree. No Christian can believe that anyone is beyond redemption. In autumn 1990, I went to Winchester to speak for a prisoner with a long criminal record convicted, though insisting on his innocence, of serious drugs offences. I was told that he might receive ten or fifteen years. In fact he got twenty-five years and a very heavy fine. It is prudent to refrain from further comment as I understand that the sentence is subject to appeal.

It should be realized that punishment in the community is in itself a complex notion. As set out above, there is to be 'greater emphasis on bringing home to the criminal the consequences of his actions, compensation to the victim and reparation to the community'. An ambitious set of proposals, and not on that account to be rejected, though there are plenty of difficulties in the conception. In Chapter V, I shall examine the whole idea of retribution or 'just deserts' as the government now wish to call it. 'An eye for an eye and a tooth for a tooth' was explicitly repudiated by Jesus Christ.

It would not be possible to represent in a brief space the reactions of penal reformers to *Crime, Justice and Protecting the Public*, but the commentary of the Prison Reform Trust goes some way to serve that purpose. They might be said to give a less than enthusiastic welcome to the government's proposals – no more than two cheers certainly, perhaps no more than one. They begin by paying a tribute:

In the view of the Prison Reform Trust, the 1990 Criminal Justice White Paper is an important step towards a more rational penal system, and one that is less reliant upon custody. Although many major issues are not addressed, both in the overall strategy and in many of its specific proposals, the White Paper is consistent with much that we and the prison reform lobby in general have been saying for many years.

However, they are soon qualifying their praise.

The White Paper is a gamble. By continuing to invest a wide discretion in the courts, the government has ceded much of *its* responsibility for planning the criminal justice system to the senior judiciary. There can be no guarantee that this gamble will come off.

They leave us with the impression that in fact they believe that the gamble will fail and that the prison population will not diminish and might even increase. Most penal reformers will sympathize with their comment on the Strangeways and other riots: 'In the light of this spring's tide of unrest in the prison system, the government's whole approach is far too timid.'

Up to this point I go along with the Prison Reform Trust. In the last paragraph of their summary, however, they seem to be avoiding the crucial issue: 'We regret that, in the general tenor, the White Paper emphasizes punishment to the virtual exclusion of any other objective of the criminal justice system.' Yet the Prison Reform Trust cannot and do not reject the whole idea of punishment in the community. Like other enlightened bodies, however, they fail to draw the distinction between punishment, a necessary element in the treatment of wrongdoers, and a punitive approach which shocks civilized people.

Is there here a distinction which is more than verbal? The government are understandably anxious to conciliate the judiciary. They are determined to prove that wrongdoers are not to be let off lightly. But they also realize that they will get precisely nowhere if they fail to conciliate the probation officers who have to administer punishment in the community. From that angle it is necessary to demonstrate that the form of punishment adopted is *constructive*. It must be in the interests not only of society, but of the men and women being punished.

There is no easy route to the striking of this balance.

IV   The Idea of Punishment

Is there an official theory of punishment?

'Our generation more than any other,' I wrote in 1961 in my book *The Idea of Punishment*, 'shrinks from inflicting pain. We are less confident than any of our predecessors in imputing guilt. The Christian ideal of forgiveness, the democrat's hatred of seeing one man held down by another, the psychologist's exposure of the element of sickness in sin and crime – all join together in our period. They cause us to look askance at the whole idea of punishment.' In 1990 I could not write in such confident terms.

The whole psychological approach to convicted criminals by the general public, by those who desire their votes and by many experts has hardened in the years between. 'The deliberate infliction of pain,' I went on, 'mental if not physical, is of the essence of punishment. So is the decision reached by one man or group of men that some other man has in some sense been guilty.' That is still as true as it was then, but the next question now seems strangely anachronistic. 'Is punishment losing or likely to lose its place in the life of our society?' Even in 1961, I admitted that there were no signs of this. There had been 11,000 men and women in British prisons and Borstals before the Second World War; by 1961 there were 27,000. Today, when there are nearly 50,000, no one is likely to suppose that punishment is losing, or likely to lose, its place in our society.

How does legal punishment come into existence at all? I ask the question logically and contemporaneously rather than historically. We can all agree that in every community professing to be civilized, there must be rules and regulations which its citizens must obey. There are, of course, many desirable rules of behaviour, moral rules and conventions, which a democratic government does not convert into laws. Any attempt to interfere with private morality past a certain point defeats its own object by interfering with human liberty so drastically that moral growth is impossible. As St Thomas Aquinas wrote: 'The commands of human law cover only those deeds which concern the public interest, not every deed or every virtue.' Some rules, however, must be enforced in an ordered society. The distinction between crime and sin will be clear from what has just been said. Sin we must leave for the moment, except to repeat that the vast majority of our sins must pass unnoticed by the State.

Crime in its broadest sense is the breach of such rules as the community decides to enforce through its penal system. To punish is defined by the Oxford English Dictionary as follows:

> As an act of a superior or of a public authority: To cause (an offender) to suffer for an offence; to subject to judicial chastisement as retribution or requital, or as a caution against further transgression; to inflict a penalty on.

The punishment with which we are concerned arises where certain rules which the community has decided to erect into and enforce as laws are broken, with a state of mind that the law decides is reprehensible. I am not concerned here with the question of what forms of conduct should or should not be made criminal, nor with the forms of penalty, though at least one of them, capital punishment, is morally intolerable.

For the purpose of this discussion I am assuming that the guilt required for a conviction and sentence, that is for legal punishment, is something close to *mens rea* in British law. The law, it should be pointed out, is not here concerned with the moral guilt of the wrongdoer. In most crimes *mens rea* means nothing more than that the person has intentionally committed the prohibited act and that he must realize that certain consequences are likely to follow from his conduct.

We will now assume that our convicted criminal stands before us in the dock. What is to be the punishment? And by referring to his punishment we are referring, of course, not only to his sentence – one year, three years, five years or whatever it may be –

but to his total treatment by the State as part of his sentence. Two men might each receive the same sentence, but might suffer or benefit very differently according to the treatment provided in prison and, let me add with emphasis, according to the after-care provided or not provided on release.

In 1961 I wrote, 'At any rate we can start from a consensus that a solution is to be found within the area of these four factors: retribution, prevention, reform and deterrence. They represent, that is to say, the outside limit. Some will deny that any place is left today for retribution.'

For a modern analysis, I will quote a passage (Para. 205) from the Carlisle Report on the parole system (1988):

denunciation	marking society's disapproval of the crime;
deterrence	both the individual deterrence of those being punished and the general deterrence of others who might contemplate crime;
incapacitation	the protection of the public through taking offenders out of circulation;
rehabilitation	the reform of the offender;
reparation	making some recompense to the victim;
retribution	exacting a penalty in proportion to the offence.

The Carlisle Committee commented on their own list (Para. 206) as follows:

The debate is usually not so much over the validity of these objectives but over the relative priority which each should command and over how they might be achieved. The importance ascribed to each of them has ebbed and flowed over time. So far, Parliament has never attempted to identify the purposes of sentencing or to prescribe the relative priority which the courts should attach to them. Instead, Parliament has chosen to give the courts an enormous breadth of discretion over the penalties for particular offences. Except for murder, mandatory custodial penalties are unknown to our statute book, and for all of the most common indictable offences the range of available penalties could scarcely be wider – anything from discharge to fourteen years' imprisonment for burglary, for example, or anything up to ten years for theft.

A comparison between the six items of the Carlisle Committee and my four given in 1961 is not difficult. Four of the items are similar to mine: deterrence, incapacitation (compare my prevention), rehabilitation and retribution. I was already becoming conscious in 1961 that reparation should be added to my list. I have since laid stress on this repeatedly in my work for victims and otherwise. It may involve recompense not only to the victim but to the State.

The remaining Carlisle item, denunciation (marking society's disapproval of the crime), arouses my intense suspicion whenever it is mentioned. It can so easily degenerate into the baying of the mob, exploited in Britain by the tabloid press and in all sorts of other ways abroad. Nevertheless, the mention of it brings up what I have long since recognized.

In discussing the views of a Home Office minister and Parole Board Chairman, Lord Windlesham, I have explained the tremendous emphasis which this high-minded man lays on public acceptance as a condition of any workable penal policy (see page 19). Public opinion, however, is not an element in a just sentence, even though in Britain or Romania, or where you will, it is in practice bound to affect what happens. In a recent well-known City fraud case the judge informed the defendant that a three-year sentence would be reduced to eighteen months because of his charity work and donations and that in view of his health he would not be sent to prison at all. The concept of just deserts must presumably be extended to cover such pleas for mitigation.

Retribution we will examine in the next chapter. At this point, let us look at deterrence and rehabilitation. If I say that no new criminological theory of deterrence has emerged in the last thirty years, that is not to deny that the many studies conducted, some of them by the Home Office, have produced conclusions of much significance, even if they are sometimes negative. The tremendous change, for example, in the attitude of the Anglican bishops to capital punishment could not have come about if they had not been persuaded by far-reaching research that capital punishment was not a unique deterrent. The public yearning for heavier sentences in the face of steadily increasing crime has been slightly, though inadequately, offset by the evidence pointing to the fact that long sentences are no more of a deterrent than short ones.

When I wrote in 1961, I insisted passionately on the necessity for a reformative element in punishment. Today the Carlisle Report treats as a matter of common knowledge the 'erosion of the rehabilitative ideal'. It gives as reasons the exaggerated hopes placed on it and the doubt cast by research on its effectiveness. To these I would add the much less sympathetic attitude of the public to prisoners in general. The Carlisle Report tries to extract something from the wreckage: 'We believe that it should be one of the prime concerns of our prisons to prepare inmates for their eventual release.'

I still cling to my earlier insistence that if far more resources, human and material, were devoted to convicted persons inside and outside prison the 'rehabilitative ideal' could be realized. The Special Unit in Barlinnie prison in Glasgow (now closed) was for a long time a model of how prisoners could be reformed. When I visited it, there were sixteen prison officers and four inmates – an impossible ratio to maintain this side of heaven, where prisons would presumably be unnecessary. Yet Barlinnie at its best gave a hint of what could be accomplished if the will for reform were there.

V Retribution

Retribution is a word of various meanings. Let me provide an illustration from the debate on Capital Punishment in 1956 in the House of Lords. The Archbishop of York had said: 'I dissent from the notion ... that it is progressive and Christian if we can gradually eliminate the element of retribution from punishment. ... I would endorse most gratefully what the Lord Chancellor has said about the moral necessity of retribution within our penal code.' The Archbishop of Canterbury had, however, spoken thus: 'The argument of retribution is brought in: that is not only clumsy, but a very dangerous argument. To defend society against murder is one thing. To repay the murderer for what he has done which is the strict meaning of retribution ... cannot be done at all. Nothing equivalent to the evil the murderer has done can ever be inflicted on him.'

When I came to speak I was bold enough to observe that the Archbishop of Canterbury had rejected retribution, while the Archbishop of York had accepted it. Both most reverend Primates at once leapt to their feet to put me right. What follows must be given in the words of *Hansard* (10 July 1956, columns 800/801).

The Lord Archbishop of York: My Lords, the noble Lord is perhaps misled by a slight difference in the use of the words. Both my fellow Prelate and myself were upholding punishment as condemnatory action by the State, to be meted out to persons who have deserved it. The most reverend Primate, the Lord Archbishop of Canterbury, was repudiating vindictive punishment and I, of course, heartily concur with him in that repudiation.

Lord Pakenham: My Lords, I am much indebted to the most reverend Primate, and I am sure that the most reverend Primate the Lord Archbishop of Canterbury would have said the same thing, no doubt, in slightly different terminology.

The Lord Archbishop of Canterbury: No, My Lords, in the same terminology.

Lord Pakenham: My Lords, I was not trying to drive a wedge between their two Lordships; no sabotage from a Roman quarter.

Was I so much misled in my original comment? Hardly, perhaps, according to the actual words that the Archbishops had used.

Be that as it may, Lord Windlesham, more than thirty years later, informs me with a good deal of authority that retribution is now a dominant factor in sentencing. I presume that he would be prepared to define it more or less precisely. It was not always so. In 1950, Lord Justice Asquith described retribution as 'a theory now so discredited that to attack it is to flog a dead horse'. A few years later Mr C. H. Rolph, as deeply versed in penal reform as anyone in Britain, congratulated the Home Secretary, R. A. Butler, on his repudiation of *savage and retributive* (my italics) penal methods. Dr George Paton, in his *Textbook of Jurisprudence* (1951), quoted with approval Professor McDougall's earlier *Social Psychology*: 'The fuller becomes our insight into the springs of human conduct, the more impossible does it become to maintain this antiquated doctrine of retribution.' McDougall added that modern criminal law must seek another basis *whatever may be the view of religion or morality* (my italics).

It is interesting to notice that the discrediting of retribution is not a mere post-war phenomenon. The late Lord Templewood pointed out when introducing the Criminal Justice Bill of 1938 that he was trying to approach these problems principally from the angles of prevention and reformation. 'In a scheme of this kind,' he said, 'there is no place for the remnants of a period that looked at the treatment of crime *principally from the angles of retribution* [my italics]. I am therefore proposing to sweep away the remnants of former dispensations, now little more than the stage properties of Victorian melodrama: penal servitude, hard labour, ticket-of-leave, the name "criminal lunatic".'

For most of this century, therefore, many people regarded retribution with horror, finding in its seemingly wicked influence all that was worst in our penal tradition. Few would be found to write in such terms today and fewer still to pen what I wrote in 1961: 'It seems indisputable that in some sense or other the retributive view of punishment was immensely stronger in the past than it is today.'

But let us pass from history and consider the issue in its present context. It is one thing to be told by Lord Windlesham and others well-placed to know that retribution is now fashionable, but is it right that this should be so?

The two main arguments against retribution are these:

1. The utilitarian principle of pursuing the greatest good of the greatest number, a principle directed solely to the future.

2. The impossibility of measuring the moral guilt of someone who has broken the law.

The late Lady Wootton, a sworn foe of the retributive principle and herself a magistrate of many years' experience, used to concede that there had to be some link between the gravity of the offence and the severity of the sentence, which is all that is necessary for a retributive element to be accepted.

As to the first argument, anyone who says that no attention should be paid to the past is really refusing to talk of punishment at all. The very idea of punishing somebody is based on the assumption that they have done something that deserved a penalty, whether or not it was actually inflicted. In practice no one, whether or not versed in penal matters, would seriously argue that there should be no connection at all of this kind. How much connection will always be a matter of dispute and will vary from tribunal to tribunal and from age to age.

I will sum up by saying that retribution provides a justification for some punishment and sets a limit to the amount of punishment justifiable. In 1961 I wrote in *The Idea of Punishment*: 'Deterrence and reform are the main factors which society should take into account in deciding how far it should exercise its right of punishment when passing sentence.' I would still make use of those words today, even though the possibilities of using prison as a reforming agency must never be discounted.

I should add that retribution is bound up with deterrence and reform because neither deterrence nor reform can perform their task adequately unless the penalty is *felt* to be just. I still feel, as I did thirty years ago, that retribution has acquired such unpleasant associations that it is high time a different word replaced it. Today, 'just deserts' is in vogue. I prefer 'fairness'.

When I first argued for a retributive element in punishment, I was swimming against the stream. I was not adopting a line which was at all popular in penal reform circles. It was associated with a rather old-fashioned form of Christianity. No longer: retribution is back in fashion. Christian principles on punishment, however, have not changed substantially. I shall be spelling out what seems to me to be the Christian approach in the next chapter.

VI Punishment and Christian Theology

The misgivings that overhang the whole conception of legal punishment can never be exorcized entirely. The modern mind – Christian or Humanist – revolts alike from the idea of unnecessary suffering and from the unverifiable assumptions involved in an imputation of guilt. Yet when we lean too far in that direction we find ourselves recalled by the juristic principles of all existing civilized societies.

Wherein lies the element of Divine punishment in Christian theology? Surely traditional Christian thinking involves the idea that the wicked suffer and rightly suffer, that all of us indeed suffer in proportion to our wickedness, of which all of us have a substantial quota? Surely, too, it is implied that this suffering, and in particular the suffering of eternal punishment, serves a useful purpose. If not, if suffering is entirely unnecessary, how can we possibly defend the theology which contains it?

A simple answer from St Augustine of Hippo can be given: 'Thou revengest that which men commit against themselves because when they sin against Thee they do so also wickedly against their own soul and their iniquity gives the lie to itself.'

The vital idea for the attention of modern man is that God punishes us only in the same measure and for the same reason that we punish ourselves. The punishment is a Divine affliction only in the sense that we ourselves are a creation of God, that we have sadly deviated from his purpose, and that when we betray the nature given us by God, the consequences work themselves out inexorably.

Divine punishment in general does not depend entirely, or perhaps mainly, on its retributive aspect. Its medicinal, its restorative, its healing function makes it an essential element in salvation. There is nothing, in fact, in the idea of Divine punishment which conflicts with modern juridical ideas, though much about it must remain mysterious, and nothing more so than the mercy which accompanies it and which we know to be infinite.

As regards the Old Testament, I will quote only one passage from a most instructive work called *Punishment in the Bible* by the Revd J. Arthur Hoyles (1986): 'To imagine that the cutting to pieces of Agag and the dashing of children against the rocks is typical of Old Testament penology is a grievous error. Shining through the variety of theological viewpoints is the base theme that God's mercy, guiding, protecting and redeeming his people, is a secure foundation for the people's gracious treatment of one another.'

But today, eternal bliss and Divine punishment cannot be discussed for long without the introduction of the Cross. And once the Cross is added, a new dimension of love comes with it. How exactly it was and is that Jesus Christ redeemed and redeems us, how, to put it crudely, the Atonement works, is too deep a subject for the present writer to expound at all adequately. The example, however, and the message to be derived from it are intelligible, and can be inspiring to all. The Gospel of Jesus Christ, in addition to what is ordinarily called its ethical content, its code of rules concerning charity, humility and other virtues, conveys a unique lesson which the story of the Cross exemplifies. We fallen human beings must 'sacrifice life to gain life'.

'The Cross gives life through death.' So said Father Leen many years ago in *Why the Cross?* Whatever else may be said about the distinctiveness of the Christian message, this particular teaching – at once metaphysical and ethical – can fairly be described as unique. 'If any man will follow me,' said Jesus, 'let him deny himself, take up his cross daily and follow me.' Suffering of itself does not transform or purify. A crucifixion can be a mere execution. But suffering accepted either as a just reward of our own sins, or on behalf of the sins of others, is equally close to the example of Christ.

A willing acceptance of vicarious suffering by a human being who is not directly to blame brings special benefits to all of us. Its acceptance by the Son of God, who is not even indirectly in the remotest degree responsible, confers on us an infinite blessing and restores, as nothing else could, our prospect of Heaven. This was and is our Redemption.

Perhaps a few further propositions may be offered in humility towards an understanding of a supreme mystery:

1. God is love. A sin is not only an offence against God, it also brings into existence an evil which can only be overcome by love.

2. Evil is the product of man's free will and can be overcome, therefore, only by a love in which man participates. In the first place there is the actual person who has committed the evil. But just as we are all sinners, all part of one human body, the love that overcomes evil can be contributed to by any member of the human race on behalf of the rest. We all believe this in our hearts instinctively, in so far as we believe at all that love can operate at a distance to strengthen those who are dear to us.

3. No act of love can be more sublime than an act of sacrifice, such as an acceptance of suffering in a spirit of love, above all vicarious suffering. Which of us does not know the feeling at a moment of sudden good fortune or worldly achievement that we ought to seek out and suffer with those in great distress? Of all acts of loving sacrifice, the gratuitous acceptance of the Cross by Jesus Christ was and must always be the most efficacious for the overcoming of evil.

One must not draw a contrast, therefore, between expiatory and useful suffering. Expiatory suffering accepted in the spirit of the Cross can perform the most useful of all services. In human beings it is combined, if accepted in that spirit, with medicinal or reformative suffering. In the case of Christ, where no sinfulness existed or improvement of character was possible, it represents pure expiation and was and is incomparably the most valuable act of suffering which has ever been performed in the history of the human race.

The greatest Christians, noticeably the saints, have understood and cherished suffering in a sense that is far beyond the capacity of the rest of us. It has seemed to them deeply rooted since the fall of man in the nature of things. Its acceptance, therefore, on their own behalf, has been the most complete way of abandoning themselves to the will of God. But let no one suppose that a Christian has any right to acquiesce more readily than a secular humanitarian in the sufferings or handicaps of others. Christ was the greatest healer of all time and he set a superhuman standard for all to follow: 'For I was hungry and you gave Me to eat; I was thirsty and you gave Me to drink; I was in prison and you came to Me. In so much as you did it to the least of these my little ones, you did it to Me.'

So the arguments are on the religious side if we take the trouble to know them and have the energy and courage to use them. But in the last resort the Christian Churches will be judged on the performance of Christians. We are watched, and it is fair enough that we should be watched very closely by our fellow men, to see whether our ethics are better, not only on paper but in ordinary life, and particularly in the face of those twin impostors, triumph and disaster.

Are we in practice more humble, more unselfish, more forgiving than those who do not possess our spiritual privileges? Who can say? It is certainly not for us to decide. But three things at least are certain. First, we shall make little headway in the advocacy or practice of our Christian principles unless we realize that without the fullest participation in Christian religious and sacramental life we are fighting God's battle with our right hand tied behind our back, and must expect to fail.

For, secondly, we are not – a thousand times not – individual, isolated Christians. There is no limit to the help which we should aspire to give one another and no limit to what we should be happy to accept from one another, knowing that where Christian fellowship is active there is no giving and taking. We are all one with another as He intends us to be one with Him and in Him.

Thirdly, referring finally to the field of punishment, our duty as Christians is not expanded or diminished according to the part we are cast for in the human drama, whether as judges, prison officers, chaplains, psychiatrists, probation officers or as others who seek to help the prisoner during and after his sentence, or indeed as prisoners ourselves.

Mr Gladstone, Acton said, gave in charge a man who tried to blackmail him, appeared in person to prosecute him, saw that he was adequately defended, visited him in prison and made sure of his employment on release. All very unpractical, it was said at the time, but as has been well remarked of it: 'What else are Christians for?'

The Christian judge, in the full knowledge that he also is a sinner like the man in the dock, judges with love and then does all he can to help the prisoner repay. And in that duty the prisoner is seen to be no lonely isolated figure – no second-class human being. For repayment is the task of us all. We should all contribute to the common pool and look to it for what we need. But the contributions are no more than Christ's merits channelled by His grace through us. Repayment is the central clue to the deepest elements in punishment and the link between punishment and the rest of human existence.

It is not the doctrinal position nor the guilt past or present which absorbs the rescue worker at that moment. It is the suffering and need of a fellow human being, and these cannot be alleviated from above or outside. When one meets a prisoner or ex-prisoner, it is not enough to say to oneself: 'There but for the grace of God go I.' One should say rather: 'There *by* the grace of God go I.' With Father Damien (of leper fame), we should move to lie down beside him and to wash his feet as those of the disciples were once washed by the hands of the Master.

VII Conclusions

Two purposes run through this book – one of universal, one of temporal and local significance. The first is to explore the nature of punishment and the essential elements in a just punishment; the second to propound a penal policy for Britain in the immediate future and the years beyond. The two purposes are intertwined. If we could clarify our ideas of punishment, we should have far more chance of carrying out the right policies.

This book was half or more written when the Strangeways prison riots occurred, followed by riots in other prisons. Nearly all the witnesses gave me their views before Strangeways, though I have no reason to think that they would alter them now. I look forward with the keenest interest to the findings of Lord Justice Woolf from his inquiry. One of his three assessors, Mary Tuck, former head of the Home Office Research and Planning Unit, gave invaluable evidence to me, but I would be surprised if any ideas laid before Lord Justice Woolf had not been mentioned in the present volume. He took the brilliant step of inviting comments from all the prison staff and prisoners in Strangeways. Again I should be surprised if he were told anything not mentioned to me by staff or prisoners in the last half century.

Earlier in this book (pages 113/14), I have summarized the proposals in *A Joint Manifesto for Penal Reform* which has been produced by the leading penal reform organizations. If carried out, they would ensure a reduction in the number of people sent to prison and in the time they spent there. They would also secure an improvement not only in the material conditions but also in the moral status of prisons. Speaking in general terms, I would support the proposals in question. But whether the aspirations of the reformers are in fact realized depends on attitudes and comprehensions among politicians, the judiciary, criminologists, social workers and the public.

No one should suppose that I am incapable of advancing beyond the positions I have assumed. My book, *The Idea of Punishment*, was published before the development of what I still call alternatives to custody, though the government do not like the phrase. As soon as it was announced as government policy, I accepted with enthusiasm the idea of punishment in the community rather than in prison. I am sure that this is, or could be, a major step forward. But everything will depend on wise and generous handling of the Probation Service. They also have their part to play in moving at least half way to meet the new vision. The government's insistence that 'just deserts' must dominate sentencing in the future is, however, crude and unconvincing. 'Just deserts' are simply, of course, retribution under another name. When I included it in 1961 among the elements of a just sentence, I was regarded as backward-looking. Now it is fashionable in official quarters. Its proper place, one of several necessary elements, has not altered.

I had hoped to include a chapter on punishment in literature, but I have not found it possible. I doubt whether anyone, however full of learning and literary insight, could discover in the greatest writers a contribution to the philosophy of punishment. In most of them there is plenty of suffering, but guilty and innocent suffer alike. None of us today would blame Oedipus for killing his father in ignorance and marrying his mother. His sufferings cannot be attributed to any acceptable system of justice. Macbeth paid the penalty for his crimes, but Lear suffered just as terribly. Dostoevsky in *Crime and Punishment* describes unforgettably the redemption of a double murderer through the love of a supremely good woman, but there is nothing theoretical there. Most of us would agree with Hardy that Tess was a pure woman, but that did not prevent her being hanged. Only in Dante perhaps might the glimmerings of a theory of punishment be discovered, but Dante in any case was concerned with punishment of man by God, not of man by man.

Dorothy Sayers, in a learned preface to her translation of Dante's *Purgatorio*, makes this claim: 'Dante has grasped the great essential which is so often overlooked in arguments about penal reform, namely the prime necessity of persuading the culprit to accept judgement.' Every judge today would, no doubt, accept such an aspiration, but taken by itself it does not carry us far towards a just sentencing policy. So great literature, regrettably, is of no help for our immediate purpose.

What in the end do we mean by punishment? In the past when I have written or talked about these matters, I have usually assumed that it included pain, but today in Britain no one beyond a few cranks is suggesting that physical pain should be inflicted on convicted persons, or even mental pain apart from restriction of liberty or economic penalties.

It is therefore simpler to think of punishment as inflicting discomfort. But many kinds of discomfort are inflicted without punishment being involved. Many thousands are incarcerated in mental hospitals without blame being attached to them. Many of us, most of us no doubt, make unwelcome sacrifices in the form of penalties. Many have been, and in other countries still are, subjected to compulsory military service and possibly sent off to die for their country. Many inflict heavy discomfort on their fellow men on the football field or in the boxing ring by mutual consent. Those like Sir Oswald Mosley who were incarcerated under Article 18B in the last war without being convicted of any crime can hardly be said to have been punished.

So punishment seems to involve a discomfort we inflict on our fellow men because in our view they have done wrong. No doubt we punish those under our own control, such as children or schoolchildren, but in this book I am concerned primarily with punishment by the State. Here we are selective. We say that some wrongdoers, notorious adulterers, for example, are not to be punished, and others are. In other words, punishment by the State is confined to those who have broken the rules which we have embodied in the criminal law.

It is difficult to believe that a State would exist for long if such rules could be broken with impunity. We are left asking ourselves what right have we imperfect, or even sinful, human beings to inflict pain on our fellow men when they break certain rules which have been promulgated in the supposed interests of society? In my view, at least, some punishment by the agencies of the State will always be necessary, if society is to exist at all. But to me the most poignant clarification which has come to me in the course of writing this book is between punishment which can be good and a punitive spirit which must always be evil. Human nature being what it is, the distinction will never be easily drawn; but it contains in my eyes the essential clue to any system of punishment based on Christian principles, or indeed on common humanity.

Punishment must by definition always be hurtful, but it should also heal. In the last resort a book about punishment should be a book, not of hurtfulness, but of healing.

Select Bibliography

The Adult Offender (London: HMSO, 1965)

Blackstone, Tessa, *Prisons and Penal Reform* (London: Chatto & Windus, 1990)

Carlen, Pat (ed.), *Criminal Women* (Cambridge: Polity Press, 1985)

Carlisle of Bucklow, The Rt Hon. the Lord, *The Parole System in England and Wales*, Cm 532 (London: HMSO, 1988)

Crime – A Challenge to Us All (London: Labour Party study group, 1964)

Crime, Justice and Protecting the Public, Cm 965 (London: HMSO, 1990)

Criteria for Custody (Briefing Paper No. 69) (London: National Association for the Care and Resettlement of Offenders, 1990)

Gate Lodge (The Magazine of the Prison Officers' Association) (London: Prison Officers' Association)

Hoyles, Revd J. Arthur, *Punishment in the Bible* (London: Epworth Press, 1986)

Johnston, Rosie, *Inside Out* (London: Michael Joseph, 1989)

A Joint Manifesto for Penal Reform (London: Penal Affairs Consortium, 1989)

Longford, The Rt Hon. the Earl of, *Causes of Crime* (London: Weidenfeld & Nicolson, 1958)

Longford, The Rt Hon. the Earl of, *The Idea of Punishment* (London: Geoffrey Chapman, 1961)

May, The Rt Hon. Sir John, *The Inquiry into the Circumstances Surrounding the Convictions Arising Out of the Bomb Attacks in Guildford and Woolwich in 1974: Interim Report on the Maguire Case* (London: HMSO, 1990)

Punishment, Custody and the Community, Cm 424 (London: HMSO, 1988)

Sentencing – A Way Ahead (London: Justice Educational and Research Trust, 1989)

Shaw, Stephen, *Conviction Politics, A Plan for Penal Policy* (London: Fabian Society, 1987)

Supervision and Punishment in the Community, Cm 966 (London: HMSO, 1990)

Tumim, Judge Stephen, *Report of Her Majesty's Chief Inspector of Prisons* (London: HMSO, 1989, 1990)

Windlesham, The Rt Hon. the Lord, *Responses to Crime* (Oxford: Oxford University Press, 1987)

Women's Equality Group, *Breaking the Silence* (London: London Strategic Policy Unit)

Wootton, Barbara, *Science and Social Pathology* (London: Greenwood Press, 1978)

Index

Page numbers in **bold** type refer to principal interviews, ideas and accounts.

access, rights of, 98
Ackner, Desmond, Baron, 161
Acton, John E. E. Dalberg, 1st Baron, 193
admonishment ('caring rebuke'), 68–9
Adult Offender, The (White Paper), 163
aftercare, 58
Allen of Abbeydale, Philip Allen, Baron, **30–8**
All-Party Penal Affairs Group (parliamentary), 79
Amlot, Roy, 118
APEX, 138
Aquinas, St Thomas, 44, 181
Armstrong, Patrick, 117
Asquith, Sir Cyril (Lord Justice), 186
Association of Chief Constables, 63
Astor, David, 14
Attlee, Clement, 1st Earl, 22
Augustine of Hippo, St, 189

bail, 172–3
Bail (Home Office circular), 172
Bail Act, 1976, 171
Baker, Kenneth, 174
Barlinnie prison, 184
Bartell, John, 59

Bedford prison, 6
Bentham, Jeremy, 42
Bettsworth, Michael, **129–31**
Birmingham prison, 6, 148
Birmingham Six, 117
Blackstone, Tessa, Baroness, 126; *Prisons and Penal Reform*, 3–6
Blake, George, 11
Bowlby, Dr John, 9
Brady, Ian, 14
Breaking the Silence (Women's Equality Group document), 126
Bristol Association for the Care and Resettlement of Offenders (BACRO), 112
Brittan, Sir Leon, 174
Brixton prison, 21, 170–1
Broadmoor, 37–8, 67–8, 169
Brockway, Fenner and Hobhouse, Stephen: *English Prisons Today*, 73
Bullwood Hall prison, 132, 136
Burt, Cyril, 9
Butler of Saffron Walden, Richard Austen Butler, Baron, 35, 174, 186
Butler Awards, 49

Canterbury, Geoffrey Fisher, Archbishop of, 185–6

Canterbury, Robert Runcie,
  Archbishop of, 3
capital punishment, 32, 35, 39,
  62–3, 183, 185–6; abolition of,
  173
'caring rebuke' *see* admonishment
Carlen, Pat (ed.): *Criminal Women*,
  122–3
Carlisle of Bucklow, Mark
  Carlisle, Baron *see Parole System
  in England and Wales, The*
Causes of Crime (Longford), 8, 13
Cavadino, Paul, **79–84**
Chancellor, Sir Christopher, 132
Channon, Olivia, 132
Chesterton, G. K., 45
child molesters, 169–70
Christianity: and punishment,
  189–93
Christie, John Reginald Halliday,
  30
Churchill, Sir Winston S., 173
Cleveland Criminology Society, 68
Colville of Culross, John Mark
  Alexander Colville, 4th
  Viscount, 19
Committee on the Prison
  Disciplinary System, 114
community service, 34, 48, 100,
  112, 156, 174–5
Conlon, Gerard, 118–19
Conlon, Giuseppe, 118
contrition, 75
Control Units (prison), 145–6,
  148
corporal punishment, 32, 35
Court of Appeal, 86–7, 96, 121,
  161–2
Craig, Christopher, 12–13
Craig, Niven, 13
crime: causes, 9–10; incidence of,
  10, 13, 40–2, 71; prevention, 62;
  violent, 62–3, 81–2, 143, 159,
  177

Crime – A Challenge to Us All
  (report), 12, 164
Crime, Justice and Protecting the Public
  (White Paper), 6, 14, 28, 44, 48,
  53, 82, 86, 91, 100, 160–2,
  173–9
Criminal Injuries Compensation
  Board, 106–7
Criminal Justice Acts: 1938, 186;
  1979, 164; 1982, 113
criminology, 39–42
Criteria for Custody (NACRO
  memorandum), 160

Damien, Father (Joseph de
  Veuster), 193
Dante Alighieri, 195
d'Arcy, Father Martin, SJ, 75
Dartmoor prison, 142
denunciation, 158, 182–3
Detention Orders, 68
deterrence, 13, 44, 80, 158, 182–4,
  187–8
diminished responsibility, 96
Disraeli, Benjamin, 28
Donaldson, Frances, Lady, 12
Dostoevsky, Fyodor: *Crime and
  Punishment*, 195

East Sutton Park open prison, 132,
  135–6
Eastwood, Alan, **61–3**, 155
electronic tagging, 59
European Convention on Human
  Rights, 99, 102
Evans, David, **57–60**
Evans, Timothy, 30
Ewart-Biggs, Jane, Baroness,
  11

Fisher, Geoffrey *see* Canterbury,
  Geoffrey Fisher, Archbishop of
Fitt of Bell's Hill, Gerry Fitt,
  Baron, 119

Fitzgerald, Edward, **96–102**, 155, 168–9
Fletcher, Harry, **89–92**
Foucault, Michel, 42
Fresh Start, 29, 55–7
Fry, Margery, 74

Gate Lodge, The Prison Officers' Magazine, 59
Gibbens, Dr Trevor, 8
Gladstone, William Ewart, 193
Grunhut, M., 8
Guildford Four, **117–21**

Hailsham of Saint Marylebone, Quintin McGarel Hogg, Baron, 155
Hardy, Thomas, 195
Hare, Gilbert, 6–7
Harris of Greenwich, John Henry Harris, Baron, 19
Higgs, Douglas, 120
Hill, Paul, 117, 119
Hillary, Edmund, 22
Hindley, Myra, 14–15, 21, 49, 168
Hoare, Sir Samuel (*later* Viscount Templewood), 31, 173–4, 186
Holloway prison, 90, 123, 132
Holtom, Christopher, **103–12**
Home Office Research and Planning Unit, 39, 75
Hood, Roger, 39
hospitals, special, 68–9, 72; *see also* Broadmoor
Howard League for Penal Reform, 73–4
Hoyles, Revd J. Arthur: *Punishment in the Bible*, 190
Hull prison, 145
human rights, 98–9
Hume, Cardinal Basil, Archbishop of Westminster, 117–18, 121
Hunt of Llanfair Waterdine, John Hunt, Baron, **22–5**, 175

Hurd, Douglas, 20, 26, 86, 174
Hutchinson of Lullington, Jeremy Hutchinson, Baron, 170

Idea of Punishment, The (Longford), 11, 36, 39, 175, 180, 187, 195
Imbert, Sir Peter, 63
incapacitation, 176, 182–3
injustice, 73
Inmate Regimes – A Service in Decline (POA report), 57
Intermediate Treatment Fund, 22

Jackson, George, 41
Jenkins of Hillhead, Roy Jenkins, Baron, 35, 164
Jesus Christ, 190–2
Johnston, Rosie, **132–41**; *Inside Out*, 132
Johnston, Susanna, 132–3, 135–6, 138–41
Joint Manifesto for Penal Reform, 79, **113–14**, 194
judges: and system, 27; lack knowledge of prisons, 31; discretion in sentencing, 61, 99–100, 161; reactionary nature, 91; and diminished responsibility, 96; as 'maimed characters', 141
just deserts, 45, 81, 101–2, 176–7, 183, 188, 195; *see also* retribution
Justice (society), 11, 158

Kee, Robert, 117
Kennedy, Ludovic, 117
Kim Wan, **142–4**
King, Roy, 2–3

Lane, Geoffrey Dawson Lane, Baron (Lord Chief Justice), 141
Leeds prison, 6, 7
Leen, Father: *Why the Cross?*, 190
Leicester prison, 6

lesbianism: in prison, 127
Leyhill open prison, 129–30
Logan, Alistair, 117
Longley, Clifford, 2

McDermott, Kathy, 3
McDougall, William: *Social Psychology*, 186
McGraw, Eric, **93–5**
McNaughton rules (on insanity), 97
magistrates, 61
Maguire Family Group, **117–21**
Maguire, Anne, 118–20
Maguire, Anne-Marie, 119
Maguire, Patrick, 118–19
Maidstone prison, 55
Masterson, John, **145–51**
Matthew Trust for Mental Patients and Victims of Crime, 67
May, Sir John, 118, 120
Mental Health Acts, 67–8
mentally disturbed offenders, 68–70, 96–9, 102, **168–70**
Milton, Frank, 8
Morris, Terence, 2, **73–8**
Mosley, Sir Oswald, 196
Mountbatten Committee on Prison Escapes and Security (1966), 35–6, 50–1
murder: and life imprisonment, **166–8**

Nathan Report on Murder and Life Imprisonment (1989), 20, 166
National Association for the Care and Resettlement of Offenders (NACRO), 7, 47, 79, 83–5, 93, 103, 138; report on criteria for custody, 160
National Association of Prison Visitors, 94

National Association of Victim Support Schemes, 105, 107
National Criminal Policy Committee (proposed), 79–80
New Bridge for Ex-Prisoners, 11, 43–5, 138
New Horizon Youth Centre, London, 13
Nuffield Foundation, 8–9, 93

Pakenham/Thompson Committee, 67
Parker of Waddington, Hubert Lister Parker, Baron (Lord Chief Justice), 32
parole, 12, 23, 46, 59, 84, 114; supervision of, 83; and life imprisonment, 167–8; introduced, 173; *see also Parole System in England and Wales, The*
Parole System in England and Wales, The (committee and report; chairman: Lord Carlisle of Bucklow), 12, 20, 23–4, 37, 46, 84, 101, **163–7**, 182, 184
Paton, George: *Textbook of Jurisprudence* 186
Patten, John, 20, 48, 53, 174
Pentonville prison, 58
police: arming of, 62
Police Federation, 61–3
prerogative of mercy, 30
Prior, Peter, 114
Prison Medical Service, 125
prison officers, 51–2, 55–6, 58
Prison Officers' Association, 50, 57–60, 63, 173
Prison Reform Trust, 85, 177–8
prison visitors, 93–4
prisons and imprisonment: British population, 4–6, 43, 86–7, 146–7, 162, 180; alternatives to, 6, 13–14, 59, 81; work and training in, 27–8, 36, 156; open,

36; theory of, 81–2; costs, 89;
women's, 90–1, 122–8, 134–8;
and human rights, 98–9; staff
attitudes, 146, 151; sex offenders
in, 149–50
Prisons and Penal Policy (NACRO
document), 79
Probation Service: and
punishment, 24–5, 112, 140;
Allen on, 34; friendliness to
offenders, 44–5, 140; and penal
reform, 89, 175, 178, 195; role,
89–90; reorganization, 91, 139;
and community punishment,
156
Profumo, John, 13
proportionality (of punishment),
159
Prosecution of Offences Act, 1985,
172
prostitutes, 99
protection (of society), 158
punishment: within the
community, 24; and young
offenders, 24–5; and training,
28; necessity of, 53–4, 75–6;
theory of, **180–4**, 196–7;
defined, 181; Divine, 189–90;
pain and discomfort in, 196

Ralphs, Enid Mary, Lady, 158
Ramsey, Michael *see* York,
Michael Ramsey, Archbishop of
rape: victims of, 108–9
Reading prison, 5
recidivist rate, 70
rehabilitation, 53–4, 83–4, 87, 92,
155, 158, 182–3
remand prisons, 59, **170–3**
remission, 59
reparation, 158, 182–3; *see also*
victims
retribution, 81–3, 158–9, 182–3,
185–8; *see also* just deserts

Richardson, Carole, 117
Rolph, C. H., 186
Runcie, Robert *see* Canterbury,
Robert Runcie, Archbishop of

Sayers, Dorothy L., 195
security, 58
Sentencing – A Way Ahead (Justice
report), 158
sentencing and sentences: and
prison population, 4–5; severity
of, and deterrence, 13, 44, 46–7,
53, 80, 158, 176, 183–4; and
training of judges, 37; and
judges' discretion, 61, 99–101,
157–8, 182–3; maximum,
100–1, 160; life, 101, 166–8;
policy proposals and
recommendations, **157–62**; *see
also* judges; just deserts
Sentencing Council, 7, 47, 79,
85–6, 91, 113, 160, 162
*Service Under Threat, A – The Future
of Probation*, 89
sexual offences and offenders,
81–2, 97, 149; and victims on
release, 104–5; maltreatment of,
149–50; and sentencing, 159,
177
Shaw, George Bernard, 45
Shaw, Stephen, **85–8**; *Conviction
Politics, A Plan for Penal Policy*, 85
Snow, Jon, 13
solitary confinement (Rule 43), 98,
129, 134, 146
Stafford-Clark, David, 8
Stonham, Victor, Baron, 21, 170
Strangeways prison, Manchester:
1990 riots, **1–3**, 60, 63, 92,
145–6, 178, 194; overcrowding
in, 6; report on, 29; sexual
offenders in, 150
stress: reduction of, 29
suffering, 189–91

suicide in prison, 7
Summerskill, Dr Edith, 146
Sun newspaper, 1, 157
Supervision and Punishment in the Community (Green Paper), 14

Tate, Tim: *Child Pornography*, 169
Tchaikovsky, Chris, **122–8**
Templewood, Viscount *see* Hoare, Sir Samuel
Thatcher, Margaret (and Thatcherism), 33, 74–5, 174
Thompson, Peter, **67–72**, 155–6, 168–9
Times, The, 169
Timms, Revd Peter, 2–3, 14, 33, **49–56**, 156
Tuck, Mary, **39–48**, 155, 176, 194
Tumim, Judge Stephen, 7, **26–9**, 31, 33, 36, 59, 130, 156

Ullswater, Nicholas James Christopher Lowther, 2nd Viscount, 161

Varillon, François: *Joie de Croire, Joie de Vivre*, 23
Victim Support Schemes, 103, 105, 109–10
victims: reparation and compensation to, 11, 106;

treatment of, 15; aid and protection for, 103–12
violent crime *see* crime

Waddington, David, 86
Wakefield prison, 50, 145, 148
Waugh, Evelyn, 12
Whitelaw, William, Viscount, 174
Widgery, John Passmore Widgery, Baron (Lord Chief Justice), 32
Wilde, Oscar, 129
Williams, Shirley, 51
Wilson, Harold (*later* Baron Wilson of Rievaulx), 12–13
Winchester prison, 3, 177
Windlesham, David James George Hennessy, 3rd Baron, 19–21, 54, 155, 175, 183, 186–7; *Responses to Crime*, 9, 19, 41
Women in Prison (organization), 122–4, 127–8
women prisoners, 90–1, 122–8, 134–8
Women's Equality Group, 126
Woolf, Sir Harry (Lord Justice), 2, 7, 29, 30, 60, 161–2, 194
Wootton of Abinger, Barbara Wootton, Baroness, 9, 12, 83, 187

York, Michael Ramsey, Archbishop of, 185